DISCOURSE CONSIDERATIONS IN

TRANSLATING
THE WORD
OF GOD

DISCOURSE CONSIDERATIONS IN
TRANSLATING
THE WORD
OF GOD

KATHLEEN CALLOW

zondervan
PUBLISHING HOUSE
OF THE ZONDERVAN CORPORATION
GRAND RAPIDS, MICHIGAN 49506

Discourse Considerations in Translating the Word of God
© 1974 by The Zondervan Corporation, Grand Rapids, Michigan

Library of Congress Catalog Card Number 74-4950

Printed in the United States of America

CONTENTS

PREFACE

This volume is a companion volume to *Translating the Word of God* by Beekman and Callow, and its contents presuppose the contents of the larger work. In particular, this volume takes for granted that an idiomatic approach to translation is being used and that the arguments presented in *Translating the Word of God* in support of that approach have been read and understood.

The particular interest of this volume, however, is in what may be termed the "discourse structure" of the receptor language. The translator knows the meaning that he has to convey in the RL — but how can that meaning be conveyed in a way that is both natural and meaningful in the RL? The following chapters provide an answer to that question.

The study of discourse structure is a relatively new field of interest in linguistics. Even so, quite a bit of material has already been accumulated. Most translators are not familiar with these developments, nor have they been applied in any systematic way to the particular needs of a translator. This volume is not an attempt to make a comprehensive survey of the field of discourse studies. Rather, it makes use of the concepts now being developed to open windows for the translator through which he may look at his language with fresh eyes. With these new perspectives, he can insure that his translation is truer to the finer meanings of the receptor language.

Kathleen Callow has worked both in Brazil and in Ghana, West Africa, and in this latter area she has helped to initiate translation work in the Kasem language, and served as a linguistic consultant. She graduated in philosophy from Glasgow University, Scotland, and also holds a degree in theology from London University.

The author wishes to express her sincere gratitude to Miss Sue Harris for typing the manuscript, to Miss Edna Jane Travis for preparing the indexes, and to Miss Betty Huizenga for checking punctuation and stylistic features. She is also indebted to her colleagues who made comments on earlier drafts, and to those who went to considerable trouble to send her materials on their languages illustrating the theory presented in this volume.

DISCOURSE CONSIDERATIONS IN

TRANSLATING
THE WORD
OF GOD

CHAPTER 1

The Organization of Discourse

INTRODUCTION

In *Translating the Word of God*, all the chapters are in some way concerned with meaning — the meaning of a given construction or word, or how such meanings may be analyzed. One main purpose of this emphasis has been to assess as accurately as possible the exact meaning of the original, for unless the meaning of the original is accurately grasped it cannot be accurately translated. In addition, if a translator has the tools for exact analysis of the meaning of the original, he also has the tools for the analysis of words and constructions in the RL, so that he can match meaning for meaning. The tools provided in *Translating the Word of God*, then, apply equally to the original languages and to the RL, and they are concerned with meaning.[1]

In this book, then, it is assumed that the translator knows the meaning of the original, or at least has available the helps and aids he needs for discovering it. With this knowledge, half the translator's problems are solved — but only half. He still has to reclothe the meaning of the original in the words and syntax of the RL. And this is no small task. It is one thing to know the propositional analysis of a passage; it is another thing to express the meaning which that analysis presents accurately and naturally in the RL. To say to a translator, "This is what the original means; now you just

[1] We are here using "meaning" in the ordinary man-in-the-street sense, of the outside-world referent signaled by speech. When we say, "What does this Greek genitive really *mean?*" we are in effect saying, "What actual events and persons is this utterance referring to?" A more accurate term, linguistically speaking, might be *content*. Halliday (1970b, p. 6) says, "An utterance must be about something," and uses the term *content* (1970a, p. 324) to describe what the utterance is about. But since most translators, in their normal speech, would call that the *meaning* of the utterance, we will use the latter term here.

9

translate it," is rather like leading a blind man half way across a busy road and then leaving him stranded in the middle; he still has to negotiate the traffic coming in the other direction. On the other hand, since every RL is different, what possible help can be given to the translator as he faces his second stream of traffic, as he seeks to recast the meaning of the original into one particular RL?

The problem facing the translator is this. He can now assess the meaning of the original, and state it accurately in the form of propositions, or use a propositional statement prepared by others. But he does not want his translation to sound like a string of propositions. No one *talks* propositions, and no one regards a propositional analysis as the most readable way to express the meaning. Propositional statements are not meant to be readable in that sense, but to provide a scientific presentation of the meaning of the original, unambiguous and accurate. Just like legal documents, they achieve unambiguous accuracy at the expense of readability. But the RL version must sound natural; how can readability and naturalness be obtained without loss of accuracy?

In any language, a person wanting to convey a message uses words, and organizes the words in ways characteristic of that language. This was true of the original writers of Scripture; they used words, and used them in ways characteristic of their languages. The translator, in trying to express the same content in another language, uses exactly the same means as the original writers did: he uses words, organized this time in ways characteristic of the RL. In the selection of the right words, principles outlined in chapters 11-13 of *Translating the Word of God* will be found useful. But when the right words are found, they still have to be organized according to the characteristic patterns of the RL: without such organization they will not even convey a message, let alone a readable and natural one.

Wilson, in comparing an old version and a revised version of the gospels in Dagbani ('Ingredients of good, clear style' unpublished ms.), says, "For a native speaker it was difficult to express what was wrong with the earlier version, except that it was 'foreign.' Since superficially there seemed to be no obvious grammatical blunders, and the vocabulary was not obviously faulty, the ingredients of this foreignness were not at first apparent. Now, however, a comparison . . . has made clear that what the older version mainly suffers from are considerable deficiencies in 'discourse structure' i.e., in the way the sentences are combined into well-integrated paragraphs, and these in turn into a well-constructed whole. The new version, on the contrary, shows native-speaker mastery over the means of signposting the text into a coherent, clear prose, which is . . . a real pleasure to read."

In this book therefore, various factors will be considered which will be of help to the translator as he seeks to discover the characteristic patterns of his particular RL, so that the message of the original may be conveyed as clearly and naturally as possible.

To a certain extent, of course, the grammar of the RL provides certain fixed patterns which must be used if any meaning is to be conveyed at all. If the noun subject always follows the verb, or if a relative clause always uses a certain verb mood, then of course the translator will use these forms. But every translator soon finds that there is more than one way of saying the same thing. He can say, "A man went down from Jerusalem to Jericho," or "There was a certain man; he went down from Jerusalem to Jericho," or "A certain man left Jerusalem to go down to Jericho," etc. The translator has to choose which is the most natural and most accurate way of conveying the information in the language concerned. This kind of choice is usually made on the basis of the reaction of native speakers, combined with the instinct of the translator. But in fact the translator does not now need to rely so heavily on instinct in such matters, as there are methods available for the study of naturalness, and by using these he can assess which of several possibilities is the best in the given context.

In this book four aspects of naturalness will be considered, which might be called "categories of appropriateness." These are not so much concerned with meaning as with the best way of expressing that meaning, and each of the four categories is relevant for any utterance Thus a translator, faced with alternative ways of saying the same thing, has four different criteria, or rather sets of criteria, which he can apply to determine which is the most suitable. These four categories of appropriateness are *grouping* (how the utterance concerned fits into some larger group, which itself functions as a unit in the discourse as a whole); *cohesion* (how participants and events mentioned in the utterance relate to other participants and events already mentioned in the discourse); *information structure* (how much information the utterance conveys, and of what kind); and *prominence* (how important the utterance is compared to other utterances in the same discourse). Grouping (above sentence level) will be considered in chapter 2; grouping below sentence level is largely determined by the grammar and this is discussed in chapter 5, part II. Cohesion, prominence, and information structure are discussed in chapters 3, 4, and 5 respectively. The remainder of the present chapter is not concerned with any particular category of appropriateness, but rather deals with a preliminary matter relevant to all of them, that of different discourse types or genres.

The relationship between *Translating the Word of God* and the various materials handled in these chapters can perhaps best be seen in terms of what Halliday (1970a, pp. 322ff) calls the three functions of language. These are:

1. The "ideational" or content function: what a given utterance is about; participants and events in certain relationships.
2. The "interpersonal" or social role function: the way in which the speaker is involved, whether as questioner, teacher, etc.
3. The "textual" or discourse function: the value or significance attaching to the utterance in the discourse as a whole.

Every utterance has all three functions simultaneously. It passes on information, implies a certain relationship between speaker and hearer, and fits into the discourse context in a certain way. *Translating the Word of God* is mostly concerned with content. Interpersonal factors are mentioned throughout the book, but are particularly relevant in the present chapter, where a major factor distinguishing different types of discourse is the relationship between speaker and hearer. The "textual" function is under consideration in the other chapters, and what we are calling *categories of appropriateness* might equally well be called, in Halliday's terms, *categories of discourse texture*.

Discourse Types

In everyday life we all use different types of speech in different circumstances. A teacher who has been teaching a class will adopt a different type of speech when she goes to be interviewed for a new appointment, and a different type again when she relaxes with friends in her apartment. A woman will refer to herself in the third person when speaking to a small child ("Mommy is just going out, she won't be long") or when writing a formal article ("The present writer considers . . .") but in virtually no other circumstances; in English the use of third person forms with first person reference is restricted to those particular types of discourse.

Not only do we use different discourse types, but we have marked reactions when a discourse type is used inappropriately. We drowse through a sermon which is read as though it were an essay in literary criticism; we inwardly scorn the lady who addresses a pet poodle as if it were a child; we chuckle at the army officer who addresses everyone with an authoritative bark.

In other words, different types of speech are appropriate in different situations. The relevant factors in the situation are primarily the relationship between the speaker and the addressee, and the nature of the message. If the speaker is exhorting the hearer to do something, certain linguistic forms will be appropriate; if he is arguing, instructing, or passing on information, other forms will be more fitting. The Scriptures exhibit several different types of discourse — narratives, letters, exhortations, requests, prophecies, and others. If a message is to come across clearly it must be appropriately worded: It is important that the translator encode each different type of message in the appropriate way. Failure to do so may in extreme cases result in the message being completely misunderstood. More often, there is the less dramatic but very serious result that the Scriptures sound awkward and unnatural, the total message does not come across clearly, and hence motivation to possess a copy, and to study it once acquired, is considerably lessened.

Major types of discourse, which show different characteristics in most languages and which are needed in translation, are the following: narrative, procedural, hortatory, explanatory, argumentative, and conversation.

Narrative discourse recounts a series of events ordered more or less chronologically, usually in the past. Procedural discourse also shows chronological ordering, but since its purpose is to give instructions as to the accomplishing of a task or achieving of an object, it more commonly employs future or habitual present tenses. Discourse types in which chronological factors have little or no significance are hortatory, explanatory and argumentative. Hortatory discourse attempts to influence conduct; explanatory discourse seeks to provide information required in particular circumstances, and often does so by providing detailed descriptions of a person, situation or activity. Argumentative discourse attempts to prove something to the hearer, and tends to exhibit frequent contrast between two opposing themes.

Sometimes in a given language, narrative and descriptive discourses are found to constitute one type; sometimes hortatory and procedural exhibit the same characteristics. But all need to be studied. No attempt will be made here to study each type separately as details are highly language-specific; rather, various factors will be mentioned which frequently differentiate one type from another, and which should therefore be borne in mind in translation.

FACTORS DIFFERENTIATING DISCOURSE TYPES

Person orientation

A major factor differentiating discourse types is their person orientation. Narrative discourse is normally told in either first or third person according to whether the narrator did or did not participate in the events narrated. In general this accords with New Testament usage and causes no problem, but fairly frequently in the New Testament a narrator will refer to himself in the third person (see section on 'Special uses of the category of person' in chapter 7 of *Translating the Word of God*). Naturally, the third person form should only be retained in the receptor language if study of text material shows that in such contexts third person form may have first person reference in the RL also.

Other discourse types diverge widely as to their use of person orientation. In Bontoc (Philippines), for example, an exhortation to perform an activity makes frequent use of the second person singular, whereas exhortation to better character prefers first person dual form for topic subject, and deletion of the pronoun altogether for non-topic subject. Explanatory discourse also shows divergences in different languages, some using second person ("you do this"), others a general third person ("people do this"), and others allowing great freedom of choice of person. Procedural text also exhibits several possible person-selection patterns. In Oksapmin (New Guinea) procedural text is so heavily goal-oriented that one need not specify the actor at all, unless it is necessary to state that certain participants do one thing while others do something else.

In many languages special sub-types of discourse, such as parables or examples, also occur characteristically with a particular person orientation. In Wojokeso of New Guinea, for example, explanatory discourse normally occurs in third person, non-future tense; where, however, a hypothetical example occurs in such a discourse both tense and person are changed, the example being given in second person and future tense. In Bahnar of Vietnam illustrative metaphors occur in the first person. Thus Mark 4:21 ("Is a lamp brought in to be put under a bushel, or under a bed, and not on a stand?" RSV) is much more naturally rendered in Bahnar, "Do I ever bring in a lamp . . . ? Do I not put it on the lamp stand?"

In analyzing spontaneous text preparatory to translation, therefore, the person orientation of the whole text, and any unexpected changes of person within the text, require careful study.

Sentence length

Most translators start off with a strong tendency to conform to Greek sentence structure, to start a new sentence where the Greek starts a new one, and to finish where the Greek finishes. In some cases, of course, this is perfectly possible in the RL, but in many more it is either impossible or unnatural. The question then arises, how long should sentences be in the RL translation? How much information should they contain? Should two short Greek sentences be combined into one long one in the RL, or should one long Greek sentence be translated by several short ones? Many factors work together in determining sentence length in a given language, of which the most important are grammatical structure, information structure (see chapter 5), and discourse type. It is probably true that in all languages there is a certain choice of sentence length available to the translator which is simply a matter of style; nevertheless, discourse type in many languages provides a strong constraint in one direction or the other.

In Gahuku of New Guinea, there are commonly many more clauses per sentence in narrative than in explanatory material — just the opposite of Greek. Kosena, also of New Guinea, reports long sentences in narrative discourse but short in hortatory, giving a somewhat choppy effect. These contrast with Kasem (Ghana), which has a preference for short, simple sentences in narrative, and longer, more complex ones in explanatory discourse. In Shipibo (Peru) quoted speech may carry a great deal of information in one long sentence, but in the narrative matrix the same information would have to be broken up into several shorter sentences. The translator concerned did not discover this until after the first draft of Mark was completed, and when he looked back over the early translation he found that "individual sentences were understandable, but many of them had too much crammed into them; they had been treated as paragraph-length quotations, and not as narrative." The contrast between the narrative matrix and quoted speech may be seen in the following verses from Matthew, translated later: "Jesus said to him, 'Having arisen and taking up your bed, go home.' And so he arose. Having arisen he took up his bed. Taking up his bed he went home." (Matt. 9:6-7).

Involvement of narrator and of person addressed

In some languages and language families the narrator's attitude or degree of involvement is expressed in every main verb. A set of affixes occurs obligatorily, indicating whether the speaker observed the events reported, knows them from hearsay, or has deduced them from evidence. This raises many detailed problems of exegesis, often most profitably discussed at workshops in the area concerned; one problem it does *not* raise is whether or not to include the narrator's involvement. This simply cannot be avoided.

A problem of a different nature is presented by those languages which optionally, but frequently, use particles or affixes that express in some way the narrator's attitude to what he is saying, e.g., its importance, truth, likelihood, etc. Often such particles defy exact translation into English; they often vary in differing discourse types; and the problem of whether and how often to use them in translation may be acute.

Obviously the over-riding consideration here is to preserve both exegetical and dynamic fidelity; that is, the linguistic form should be natural, and should at the same time express accurately the meaning of the original. If the linguistic form is to sound natural then such "attitudinal" particles should be used only in the appropriate discourse type, and with approximately the same frequency as in that type. Particles suited to exhortation may be quite unsuited to narrative; within narrative itself, particles suited to the introduction may be quite inappropriate to the climax. Sometimes such particles have to be included in the translation if the audience or reader expects them so strongly as to be confused or misled by their omission (see chapter 5). Exegetical faithfulness here requires a very careful assessment as to what information is implied in the original. Sometimes the very fact that the narrator is presenting an argument, telling a story, or expressing surprise, is in itself a sufficient implication that such attitudinal particles are required. The entire purport of the passage might be missed by the reader were they omitted. But naturalness as such is never a sufficient reason for including such particles if they convey a meaning, or overtones, not implied in the original.

Cashinawa (Peru) has a range of verbal affixes indicating certainty or uncertainty on the part of the speaker; another set of affixes indicate degrees of insistence when imperatives are used. Both sets of affixes are of frequent occurrence in conversation, and must be used correspondingly frequently in the translation, otherwise the reported conversations in Scripture will sound flat and unnatural. Thus Genesis 1:29 reads, "Look, all the vegetables that have seeds, which are certainly all around, each of those vegetables with seed I certainly give you them. The trees which have fruit and their fruit has seed, I certainly give you them; you are to eat (focus) them." Where uncertainty is implied in Scripture it must also be expressed in Cashinawa by such affixes, as in John 20:2. "'They have taken our Lord's body from the tomb. Where have they laid him (uncertainty)?' she said to them."

Languages also vary in the frequency with which they introduce the person addressed, in conversation, exhortation, and letters. In Aguaruna of Peru, for example, vocative forms are common in conversation and in letter-writing. Paul's Greek epistolatory style does not use the vocative as frequently as does Aguaruna, hence readers tended to forget that it was a letter which they were reading. In fact, vocatives had to be introduced into the translation of Colossians at several points, partly to keep the readers aware that it is a letter, and partly to soften Paul's use of the imperative, which would have sounded harsh in Aguaruna without an accompanying vocative — and Paul was not speaking harshly.

Other factors which often function contrastively in different discourse types are paragraph structure and tense. These will be considered in chapters 2 and 3 respectively.

CONVERSATIONAL DISCOURSE

Conversation differs from the other types in that more than one speaker is involved; it is very varied, in that it may have the characteristics of any other type (argumentative, hortatory, etc.) or may be more informal than all of these. Conversational discourse does not occur as such in the New Testament, but it occurs very frequently embedded in a narrative matrix, and also in an argumentative type matrix.

Conversational discourse presents a special challenge to many translators because of the different ways in which languages handle quotations. Problems cluster around two major factors: first, whether to use direct or indirect quotation; and second, how to refer to the different participants so that it is unambiguously clear who is meant.

In some languages, either direct discourse ("He said, 'I will come tomorrow'") or indirect discourse ("He said that he would come next day") is mandatory. There is no other way of saying it. Sometimes direct speech must be used when it is only implied in the original. For example, in many languages of the Americas, and in Australia and New Guinea, direct quotation is used even in the expression of thoughts and opinions, or to convey the attitude of the speaker. Greek and the European languages are rich in words which imply the attitude of the speaker, for example "accuse," "rebuke," "desire," etc. Other languages convey the same information by using the verb "say," and following it with a direct quotation which contains some definite feature indicating the manner of speaking. For example, in Gugu-Yalanji (Australia), Mark 5:37, which contains only implied speech in the original (". . . he allowed no one to follow him except Peter and James and John") has to be translated using direct speech, thus, "He said, 'Peter, James, John, you come with me. Nobody else come.'" (See Moore and Turner, NOT 24:1-35; also Edgerton, NOT 10:7, 8.) It is important to note that the same content is conveyed here as in the original; it is simply that the forms available in Gugu-Yalanji compel a transfer of some of that content from a narrative form to a direct quotation form.

Problems of a different sort arise when a language has both direct and indirect quotation forms, but uses them in different ways from the original. Many direct quotations in the Scripture are quite lengthy, (for example, Jesus' teaching in Matthew 23) but some languages would more naturally use indirect quotation for lengthy passages. Others, such as the Gur language of West Africa, can slip quite naturally from direct to indirect speech in the middle of a long quotation, without any indication other than the change of pronoun referent. Some languages need the occasional insertion of such phrases as "Jesus continued and said . . ." so as to make it clear to the readers that a long quotation is still continuing. In other languages (for example, Bariba of Dahomey) there are very complex rules as to whether direct or indirect quotation should be used. (See Pike, 1966, pp. 86-92.) In that language, for instance, if a preacher says, "Jesus said, 'I am the way, the truth and the life,'" the hearers' expectation of indirect quotation is so strong that they will interpret the quoted direct speech as indirect, and assume that Jesus' original statement was that *the preacher* was the way, the truth and the life. This is a rather extreme example of an all-too-common phenomenon — the misinterpretation of the person referred to by pronouns, when the normal quotation forms of the language are not used.

CHAPTER 2

Grouping

Within a discourse, the content is not presented in an undifferentiated stream, like an inventory or shopping list. Whatever is to be said is grouped, so that related material is together, and the relationship of the groups to each other may be seen. Sometimes a grammatical construction itself, e.g., a particular sequence of clauses, carries certain implications about the grouping of the material reported, and this will be discussed briefly in chapter 5. But grouping of larger amounts of material also occurs, and will be considered here under two headings, grammatical and dramatic (plot-related) grouping.

GRAMMATICAL GROUPING

Grammatical structure does not stop at the clause. Commonly, both sentence and paragraph may be found as well-formulated units larger than the clause, and sometimes paragraphs themselves are grouped to form episodes, the latter then combining to form the total discourse. This highly regularized pattern, however, must not be taken to apply to all languages, nor even to all discourse types within any one language. To the translator, the important thing is to discover which groupings form clearly marked structures in the RL, and how they are used. Obviously, if a language has well-marked paragraph structure, for example, then a translation which ignores this structure will be confusing or even misleading to the reader. Here the grammatical units most commonly involved — sentence, paragraph and episode — will be considered in that order.

19

The sentence

In many languages, and indeed in many areas of the world, identifying the sentence as a unit causes little or no problem. In fact, the familiarity of the sentence in Indo-European languages predisposes the translator to expect to find sentences wherever he goes. In this, however, he may be disappointed. In some parts of the world the sentence as a unit is a bit too nebulous for convenience. In Mantjiltjara (Australia)[1] for example, there is no clear unit between clause and paragraph, and the discourse flows along mostly by juxtaposition. But it would be a mistake to think that such languages are deficient in structure; rather, the structure lies not in the grammar but in the information-content (see chapter 5) and the grammar may be adequately handled by having one unit between clause and discourse, whether it be called sentence or paragraph. In such cases the translator has to express the Scriptural message in the most natural way conveying each kind of information in the appropriate form.

In other languages the sentence as a unit occurs in some discourse types and not in others. In Waffa (New Guinea) the sentence is clearly marked in explanatory and hortatory discourse, and sentences build up into paragraphs equally clearly. In third person narratives, however, the sentence is nowhere to be found, or rather, the distinction between sentence and paragraph disappears; one may only say that all narrative paragraphs consist of one sentence, and that the sentence can be quite long.

In languages in which the sentence is a distinct unit, the translator still faces the problem of how much information to put into one sentence, and when to start a new one. Sometimes this is determined by purely grammatical criteria. For example, it may be that a purpose clause, or a quotation, always ends a sentence. But often the grammar provides no such determining factors; it would

[1] We are grateful to our colleague, Dr. R. E. Longacre, for drawing our attention to the Mantjiltjara material, and for giving us access to his findings, prior to publication, in several Australian and New Guinea languages. Dr. J. E. Grimes gave similar assistance with prepublication materials from Brazil, and Dr. Beatrice Clayre gave access to private notes on Philippine and Malaysian materials. Most of the actual examples quoted in these chapters, however, were provided by fellow-translators who took time and trouble to answer specific queries by correspondence. In view of the type of source used, bibliographical evidence has been provided only where an exact quotation is made from published or submitted material. Where no bibliographical evidence is provided, it may be assumed that the information came directly from the translator concerned.

be equally possible, grammatically, to continue the original sentence or to start a new one. At this point factors come into play which are dealt with in more detail in later chapters. Commonly, changing to a different participant as subject necessitates starting another sentence. Sometimes there may be no change of agent, but if the original participant changes objective, this may make a new sentence necessary. Sometimes the question of sentence length may be determined more by information factors; a sentence may naturally convey a certain amount of information and no more (see chapter 5).

The above is sufficient to show that in questions of grouping (i.e., how much information to put together into one sentence, and how to group these sentences into larger units), no one factor alone is decisive. But since information is expressed by the use of grammatical patterns, the translator needs to have some awareness of the nongrammatical factors which combine to determine the use to which a given grammatical unit is put. The ordering of sentences within a larger group is discussed at the end of chapter 3, while the amount and kind of information conveyed by a given grammatical construction are discussed in chapter 5.

The paragraph

The paragraph has been thoroughly investigated in numerous languages over recent years, and no attempt will be made here to cover the large amount of material now available. Instead, suggestions will be made which should provide lines of investigation for a translator wishing to launch into paragraph studies on his own, and examples will be given of the way in which paragraph structure is relevant in translation.

Normally there are several common paragraph patterns in a given language; these are often related to discourse types. Thus a narrative paragraph will often exhibit different structure from an argumentative paragraph, or a hortatory one from an explanatory one. This is by no means rigid, however, and a paragraph with the basic characteristic of contrast, or parallelism, or comparison, etc. may occur with little variation in several discourse types.

Early paragraph analysis will start by investigating stretches of material which seem clearly to constitute one larger-than-sentence unit. When the structure of these is analyzed, it may then be used as evidence in evaluating other potential paragraphs which initially were less clear.

Paragraphs often start with a topic sentence, which acts as a setting for the paragraph as a whole, or links the paragraph to the rest of the discourse, or both. Often the topic sentence indicates a change in temporal or locational setting, a change of the participant in focus, or a preview of the argument or activity of the paragraph.

The topic sentence is often distinct, grammatically, from the rest of the paragraph. In Bororo (Brazil) the topic sentence is usually short. If particular emphasis is to be put on a new participant, the name of the participant may be put first, then repeated as the subject of the topic sentence. In Bahinemo (New Guinea) the paragraph opens with a clause containing a dependent verb, the rest of the paragraph consisting of a string of independent clauses. In Saramaccan (Surinam) the topic sentence of one paragraph type is repeated more or less exactly in the initial clause of the first event sentence, which is introduced by a special connective. Thus a Bible story in that language contains a paragraph starting, "He went and prayed to God until he finished. — Connective — He prayed to God until he finished, until all those five thousand people every one of them scattered to his house."

It is obvious that the beginning of a paragraph, though marked differently in these three languages, is in each case marked very clearly. In some cases, however, the situations which initiate a new paragraph differ from those in the Greek, and in such cases special care is needed. In Daga (New Guinea) a new paragraph is marked by change of actor, or of temporal or locational setting, or by movement from one place to another. Often this fits in well with the Greek. For example, the paragraphs beginning at John 3:22 and 6:1 contain both a temporal expression and a statement of movement from one place to another, and hence are marked as being paragraph-initial in both Greek and Daga. But occasionally a sentence that obviously starts a new paragraph in the Greek is inadequately marked from the Daga point of view; it is too abrupt. Thus John 1:6, though it contains a new actor ("a man sent from God") does not carry any sufficient indication, to a Daga speaker, that the previous paragraph (about the Word) has ended and a new one is beginning. So in the Daga translation of v. 6 a general time-word, which frequently introduces paragraphs, is inserted, and the reader is alerted that a change of topic occurs here.

A problem also arises in Daga in precisely the opposite situation, where the Greek contains in the middle of a paragraph a signal which in Daga marks paragraph-initial. This happens in Luke 10:35, in the story of the Good Samaritan. In the middle of a paragraph we find a time-word sentence-initial — "On the morrow when he departed." Obviously the reference to "the morrow" cannot simply be omitted, but some way must be found of indicating that the same paragraph is continuing and the theme is unbroken. The device used in Daga to provide this continuity is repetition. The translation of the end of v. 34 and the beginning of v. 35 now reads ". . . he cared for him. Having cared for him, on the morrow . . ." This has the double effect of providing continuity and of removing the time-word from initial position, thus solving the problem.

Cohesion within the main body of a paragraph is signaled differently in different languages. Some languages have the same participant as subject throughout, others have the same verb tense; some use connectives, others use constant repetition. In Fore of New Guinea, all the verbs in a paragraph are in "medial" mood, except the last, which has "final" mood. Ampale, also of New Guinea, uses repetition. Thus Mark 6:17-18, reordered into chronological sequence as Ampale structure demands, reads, "Before, Herod married his brother Philip's wife. *He married her*, and John kept saying to Herod, 'Taking your brother's wife is immoral.' *He said that* and . . ."

In narrative paragraphs cohesion tends to be provided by unity of participants, and by chronological sequence, however signaled. In other types of paragraphs sentences are connected in different relationships: by parallelism (related statements in the same semantic domain), by paraphrase (the same thing said twice, with or without slight changes of wording), or by logical relationships such as reason or result. Some of these will be further considered later.

Whatever the basic structure of the paragraph, it may always be interrupted by embedded materials, interpolations, etc. These also will have their own characteristic structure, hence no confusion arises. Certain signals mark interpolated material, other signals mark a return to the main flow of the paragraph. Consequently in Daga, when it seemed that the unity of the paragraph was being broken up by frequent quotations, it was restored by the same device as before — repetition. Thus John 21:16 reads, "He said to him the second time, 'Simon, son of Jonas, lovest thou me?' *He said that*, and Peter said to him, 'Yea Lord . . .'"

Sometimes an interpolation occurs in Greek unmarked by any special signal; a literal translation in such instances would be con-

fusing in any language which expected such extraneous material to
be clearly marked. In Nung of Vietnam the translation of Mark
15:38 created a problem. Verse 37 has described how Jesus died,
v. 38 describes the rending of the curtain in the temple, and v. 39
tells of the centurion's reaction to Jesus' death. In one sense v. 38
is not a digression; it is obviously closely related to the death of
Christ. From the Nung point of view it would seem a digression,
however, because Nung paragraph structure observes strict unity
of location, and v. 38 involves a change of location. When these
verses were translated as they stood, reading straight through as a
single paragraph, it was assumed by the language helper that no
change of location was involved. This seemed quite logical; presumably the centurion could see the curtain splitting, and this was
what convinced him that Jesus was the Son of God. Rather than
making the interpolation explicit by saying specifically that the
curtain was out of sight from the place of crucifixion, the translator
inverted the order of v. 38 and 39, so that the centurion's reaction
followed straight on from the death of Christ which caused it, and
the change of location occurred paragraph-final where it was correctly understood. In such instances as this, it is obviously essential
to know both how the unity of a paragraph may be maintained, and
how extraneous information may most naturally be included.

Frequently, paragraphs end with a terminal sentence. This may
state the successful attaining of his object by the main participant,
or may summarize the situation reached, or may simply consist of
the final event of a series. Sometimes it consists of an explanation
or comment, or some such material which as it were steps aside
from the main flow of the paragraph. The terminal sentence is
differently marked in different languages. In Cashinawa (Peru)
there is a paragraph-final suffix which in most circumstances, clearly
definable, means that the next agent will be a different one and a
new paragraph is about to start. In Kasem (Ghana) the terminator
of an explanatory paragraph normally summarizes the situation now
reached, and has an imperfective verb. In Kanite and Kosena of
New Guinea, as well as in Fore mentioned earlier, the end of a
paragraph is marked by a verb in "final" mood in the last clause.

When the transition from one paragraph to the next is normally
clearly marked in a language, it is obviously confusing to the reader
if the translation does not provide such signals — he does not know
for certain whether the verse he is reading is continuing the old
topic or starting a new one. In complex materials he may even

lose sight altogether of what the topic is. Yet often the solution is quite simple. In Kosena (New Guinea) the transition from God's promise to Abram in Genesis 12:3, to the new paragraph in v. 4 (Abram's departure from Haran), was unclear. In that language a new paragraph often starts by repeating in nonfinal form the verb which occurred finally, in the previous paragraph. This was done here, and the situation clarified, thus, " 'Those who do you good I will do good to them. Those who do you bad, I will do bad to them,' he said (final verb). God said that (nonfinal verb), and Abram left Haran . . . ."

The episode

Several languages exhibit a unit which can be called the episode, which is smaller than the discourse, and consists of paragraphs. Evidence so far has been found only in narrative discourse, but it is to be anticipated that current research will produce material from other discourse types also. In Ayoré (Bolivia) the episode is the unit within which one focus is maintained. There are two particles in Ayoré which indicate an impending change of focus, and an episode normally ends with a clause containing one of these, and with a short summary. The next episode begins either with a new temporal setting, or with background information, and has a different participant or situation in focus. Obviously, in translation, it will help the reader greatly if such changes of focus are signaled in familiar ways; conversely, it will confuse the reader considerably if a change of focus in fact occurs in the subject matter, but goes by unsignaled.

Nambiquara (Brazil) reports similar units (called "local themes" by Kroeker in Grimes, 1972a, pp. 351-362), which build up into narrative. Each such episode usually starts with a temporal or locational setting, and a thematic marker with a particular suffix occurs throughout the episode as new details are added. The same thematic marker with a different suffix indicates the end of the episode.

Munduruku of Brazil also has well-marked episodes, exhibiting a thematic unity centering upon one main participant who has one over-all objective throughout the episode. A change of objective means the start of a new episode, and this is clearly marked in the grammar by means of certain connectives, particles, and word order. Munduruku speakers are sensitive to this factor of the over-all objective, and an early translation which inadvertently signaled change of objective too frequently proved highly confusing to them.

In such a situation, where the structure of the RL is dependent on a factor not overtly signaled in the original, the translator has to go back to the original and virtually look at it through Munduruкú eyes, assessing who is the main participant, what is his over-all objective, and where he changes his objective. Only then is he in a position to translate the passage so that it will be clear and coherent.

DRAMATIC (PLOT-RELATED) GROUPING

Instead of considering a discourse as a purely grammatical entity, consisting of ordered patterns of sentences and paragraphs, it is possible also to consider it as a drama or plot. In this case, the units are not determined by grammatical criteria, but by their significance within the story or argument as a whole. Thus in many instances the introduction may be clearly distinguished from the main argument, while within the argument itself there is a distinction between complication/conflict (the period of problem or conflict), climax, resolution, and evaluation. Digressions within a major theme, or interwoven minor themes may also be discerned. These various elements in discourse may also be found in discourses in Scripture. Of course, terminology varies, but many commentaries contain such statements as the following: "In summing up, Paul seeks to . . ." (evaluation), "The apostle breaks off the narrative suddenly . . ." (digression), "This is the crucial passage of the Epistle" (climax), "In John's gospel this incident marks the climax of the public ministry of Jesus" (climax within one major theme), etc.

Of course, grammatical boundaries often coincide with plot-related boundaries; the introduction may consist of one paragraph, the start of the main argument may coincide with the beginning of an episode, etc. But it cannot be assumed that the two kinds of boundaries will coincide in this way. For example, Paul often seems to end one thought-unit and start another in the middle of a sentence. Even where the boundaries do coincide, grammatical units and plot-related units require separate consideration, since they are often marked by different kinds of signals.

Dramatic analysis of a discourse, although interesting at a theoretical level, would be of little concern to the Bible translator were it not that a significant number of languages signal different parts of the plot in different ways. Speakers of these languages use certain devices to signal climax, digression, etc., and conversely, when they hear these signals they interpret them as signaling climax, etc., even if that was not what the unwitting translator intended.

The introduction typically introduces the main participants and establishes the setting. Sometimes, as in Mundurukú (Brazil) it also gives a preview of some aspect of the story, in this case the major element of conflict. Another language that gives a preview of the story in the introduction is Eastern Otomí of Mexico. So strong is the Otomí expectation of a preview that if none is given, whatever is said first will be interpreted as a preview, i.e., as establishing the main theme of the story. Thus an early translation of the Christmas story from Luke was interpreted as meaning that rulers have the right to hold a census, and that people should cooperate in it as Joseph and Mary did — this was what was mentioned first, in Luke 2:1-3. Another passage misinterpreted by the Otomís for the same reason was John 2:1, 2, the story of the marriage at Cana. Otomí readers assumed that it was Jesus who was getting married, since Jesus' mother and Jesus are the first two people mentioned.

Naturally, ways may be found in Otomí of orienting the reader correctly to the discourse. But the translator first must be aware that there is a problem before he can rectify it. And it is possible for translators to remain unaware of such a problem for some time, until repeated checking reveals repeated misinterpretation.

The climax of a story, though less likely to cause misunderstandings than the introduction, is often marked by stylistic factors which the alert translator may put to good use. In Ilianen Manobo (Philippines), for example, there is a marked change of pace as the climax approaches. A story often starts very deliberately, with frequent use of connectives, but changes near the peak to a much crisper, more direct style. There is a noticeable lack of conjunctions and heavy connectives, and these are replaced by frequent use of direct quotation, and of interjections such as "Behold." Shifts of person and tense are also possible.

Fore of New Guinea uses tense to signal not chronological progression but dramatic progression within a narrative. The main body of a story is in the far past tense, but when approaching the peak, it shifts to past tense, and at the denouement changes to present tense, returning finally to far past tense for the end of the narrative.

The conclusion of a discourse also frequently has a characteristic style. In Aguaruna (Peru), for example, a story often ends with a passive construction (Larson, NOT 17, pp. 1-25). This means it would be quite natural in Aguaruna to use a passive construction in a concluding summary statement in parables or narratives. It also means it might be misleading to use a passive in the middle of a narrative; the reader might well think the story was finished at that point.

CHAPTER 3

Cohesion

We have seen that discourse does not convey information in an unvarying succession, but in groups, and that these groups are either grammatical or dramatic in structure. But grouping is not in itself sufficient to account for the patternings which we find in discourse, and which we must reproduce in translation. Imagine, for instance, a discourse consisting of six or ten well-marked paragraphs, signaled by the usual initiating and closing particles, but mentioning a new participant every sentence and never mentioning a single participant twice. Such a conglomeration of unconnected material could not possibly be called a discourse; at best it would be a list, at worst a caricature of normal speech.

Or consider a different possibility, a discourse with one or two identifiable characters throughout, but no obvious progression in their activities, just a jumble of events. A short example of such a discourse may often be found in a child's workbook as an exercise in comprehension. First come instructions: "Rearrange the following sentences in the correct order." Then follows a series of pictures with a sentence alongside each. "Then she bandaged up her doll." "First she gave some medicine to her teddy bear." Soon the patients were all better." "Mary decided to play nurse." In giving such an exercise to children in the early grades at school, we assume they already have some sense of meaningful order in the recounting of events, and we seek to develop that sense to the point of conscious control. Even a small child realizes that the disordered series of sentences does not constitute a proper discourse in the way the correctly reordered series does.

Thus we can see that discourse must exhibit not only grouping, but cohesion. It must have identifiable persons or objects which

29

form the subject matter throughout, and these persons must perform or experience a series of events in a way that constitutes an orderly progression. Our translation must likewise have cohesion, thus defined. It must be clear what participant performs each action, and in what order the various actions occur. Although this may seem very simple and elementary, it is nevertheless true that in some languages the correct identification of participants and ordering of events has caused the translator acute problems. Each language has its own patterns to convey the interrelationships of persons and events; in no language may these patterns be ignored, if the translation is to be understood by its readers.

At the outset it must be understood the term "participant" does not mean the same as "noun subject," "pronoun object," or any other grammatical designation. In the English sentence, "John took a second helping, and afterwards regretted it," the first clause has a proper noun, "John," as subject, while the second clause has no subject expressed at all. Yet any English speaker knows it was John who did the regretting as well as the eating: John was the participant involved in both events. In other words, every event has at least one participant involved in it (the one who initiated or experienced it) whether or not that participant is mentioned in the grammar. Note, however, that if the participant is not overtly mentioned, as above, it is nevertheless still perfectly clear who is referred to. The conventions of the language are conformed to by all speakers, and they know that, in English, if a clause occurs without a subject, the person who was the subject of the previous clause is understood as the subject of this clause also. However, if the rules of the language are ignored, confusion immediately results. Take the quasi-English sentence, "Tom and Bill had a fight; he kicked, he punched, he gave a black eye, until finally he ran away." This sentence does not refer to the participants according to the accepted patterns of English; the subject pronoun "he" could refer to either Tom or Bill, and no personal object is mentioned at all. The result is that we have no idea who did what. Obviously, such confusion is something which must be avoided in translation — and it can only be avoided if the Scriptural message is worded according to the accepted patterns of the language concerned.

Lest this danger seem to be exaggerated, let us consider the experience of one translator as he himself reports it. Speaking of problems that arose while revising the gospel of Mark in Shipibo (Peru), Lauriault (1957, pp. 166ff) says, "The . . . problem was to keep proper track of all the subjects and objects and possessives throughout the whole translation. Many times I found that using a pronoun where Spanish or Greek had a pronoun made the particular subject, object, or possessive refer to somebody else. Either I had to use no pronoun at all, or else use the noun . . . . Many times, as I would hear the Shipibos speak, I would get mixed up as to whom they were talking about in a particular sentence." It took him several months of work to solve his problem, and in the process he uncovered a highly complex but completely consistent system for referring to participants. Of course, not all languages are so difficult in this respect, but many are, and even the languages with a "simple" system of participant reference reserve one or two pitfalls for the unwary. If it takes some months to solve these problems, as in Shipibo, then they are months well spent.

LEXICAL COHESION

Obviously, the relationship between different participants and events is much more obvious to the reader if the words used are already known to be related, or if the same words are used several times. Thus if the word "mother" is used, a later mention of "child" will already be half expected, and readily followed. Selection of vocabulary items from a common semantic area contributes greatly to discourse cohesion. If many of the words in a paragraph come from the same semantic domain they contribute to the unity of that paragraph, and hence to the ease with which it is understood.

An example is found in Mark 1:16-20, where the nouns involved[1] are, "sea (2), Galilee, Simon (2), Andrew, brother (2), fishermen (2), Jesus, men, nets (2), James, son, Zebedee (2), John, boat (2), father, hired servants." Thus in this paragraph, disregarding proper nouns, the words "sea, fishermen, nets, boat," are related semantically, as are "brother, son, father." In addition to grammatical cohesion provided by pronouns, case endings, etc., the paragraph exhibits lexical cohesion also.

By contrast, Jude 5-7 provides much less lexical cohesion, the nominals in that paragraph being, "you, all things, Jesus, people, land, Egypt, angels, estate, habitation, judgment, day, chains, darkness, Sodom, Gomorrha, cities, manner, flesh, example, fire, vengeance." Notice that no noun occurs more than once in this paragraph, and that relatively few of the nouns belong to a common semantic domain, unless prior Christian teaching had conditioned

[1] Numerals following a noun indicate the number of occurrences.

readers to see connections between such items as *chains, darkness, fire*. The translator has to translate the lexical items found in the original; where, as here, these do not contribute to cohesion, the translator needs to take special care that grammatical cohesion is adequate.

In the rest of this chapter we will consider, first, various problems involved in referring to participants, and later, problems involved in recounting events.

COHESION OF PARTICIPANTS

Introducing participants naturally

We are all familiar with the time-honored formula, "Once upon a time there was a _____," and we have no difficulty in finishing the sentence with a description of the major character in some favorite nursery story. Other discourse types may function differently, but as far as nursery tales go, that is the right and proper way to introduce the main participant. Other languages also have their own "right and proper ways" for introducing participants into a narrative, whether at the beginning or in mid flow. Most languages have several different ways of introducing participants, and the translator must be able to use each in the appropriate context.

In English a participant is normally introduced by a noun phrase, with or without a proper name; thereafter he is normally referred to by a pronoun, at least in the immediate context. Thus we can say, "There was once a man called Peter; he did this, then he did that," and so on. But for the Bororos of Brazil this would leave Peter very inadequately introduced; in their language the new participant is referred to by a noun several times in succession before the narrator shifts into using pronominal forms.

Many languages use certain clause types, and only those clause types, for introducing participants. Bacairi (Brazil), for instance, identifies a new actor with either a special kind of noun phrase, "he, an old man," or with an equative clause, "he is an old man." This only holds, however, if the old man is entering the discourse as a major participant. If instead, he is entering as a minor actor, a third construction is used, and if he is not an actor at all, but merely the recipient of the actions of others, then a fourth constructon is used. Obviously then, the Bacairi translation has no alternative but to present every participant as major or minor — the Bacairi expect to be told, and their grammar tells them. Nomat-siguenga (Peru) also distinguishes between major and minor characters in a story, but in a very different way. In that language the main participant must be the first one referred to by a noun; other participants may be mentioned earlier, but they may only be referred to by pronominal affixes until after the main character has arrived on the scene. The fact that the use of a noun at the beginning of a story signals a participant as major is obviously important to bear in mind in translation.

Many languages resemble Bacairi and Nomatsiguenga in distinguishing between major and minor participants. Often there are special formulae for introducing major participants, but minor participants may just appear in the story unannounced. In some languages, however, no participant may appear unexplained, not even a minor one. Since Greek often slips in a minor participant without comment, a literal translation would be confusing at this point. For instance, Mark 3:11 reads, "And whenever the unclean spirits beheld him , . . ." But in Gugu-Yalanji (Australia) this sudden introduction of the unclean spirits was too abrupt. It was not obvious to the readers that the spirits were in the people among the crowd. So the translator had to introduce them properly at the beginning of the verse, "Some people had bad spirits in their heads." Then the situation was clear.

Tracing a participant through the discourse

Once a participant has been suitably introduced, it still remains to refer to him correctly thereafter, and to make sure that it is always clear who performed each event. Hebrew is rather unusual in the readiness with which it uses proper names to trace participants through a discourse. In Genesis 42:6-9, for instance, note the frequency with which the name "Joseph" occurs. "Now Joseph was governor over the land; he it was who sold to all the people of the land. And Joseph's brothers came, and bowed themselves before him with their faces to the ground. Joseph saw his brothers . . . . Thus Joseph knew his brothers, but they did not know him. And Joseph remembered the dreams which he had dreamed . . . ." This device which provides cohesion in Hebrew would sound very unnatural in most languages, and would cause complete confusion in some. In many languages a useful rule-of-thumb is to use a pronoun, after the first introduction is completed, unless at some point confusion would result, when a noun may be used. But even this simplest of cases is not without its hazards. Do you use a free pronoun or a pronominal affix or both? Where there is a danger of confusion between two or more characters, is this resolved by the use of a proper name, a demonstrative, a generic term, or possibly a descriptive noun phrase? There is no way to discover the natural usage except by careful analysis of spontaneous text in the RL. By tracing different participants through the narrative in turn it is possible to discover the normal method of referring to a previously-mentioned participant. Then the less usual forms of reference may be studied to see in what contexts they are found, whether to resolve ambiguity, to start a new paragraph, to provide contrast, or whatever.

In Nomatsiguenga, once a participant has been introduced, later references may give further details. If a very generic term such as "a certain man" was used in the introduction, then a later reference may give a more specific description. If the first mention of the participant used a kin term such as "the boy's father," then a later reference may add his name. In some languages, however, this would not be possible: all description must be stated at the outset, and further description is only possible if the situation changes in some way.

In Shipibo (Peru), once a participant has been introduced by a noun as subject, verbs usually carry on without any overt subject as long as the same participant is the agent. However, the same noun may be used again, with a demonstrative, thus, "The men did this, thus and so; then *those men* . . . ." But this repetitive nominal is only used when there is a development in the situation or activity.

A common way of referring to a known participant is by his role, whether this be his family relationship ("the father," "the firstborn"), his nationality ("the Hebrew"), his social position ("the visitor"), his official position ("the ruler"), or whatever is appropriate in the context. Pame of Mexico, for instance, makes frequent use of such terms, hence it is used very naturally in translation. For example, Acts 16:38 reads in the King James Version (following the Greek), "And the sergeants told these words to the magistrates: and they feared, when they heard that they were Romans." The three uses of "they" seemed ambiguous, though in Greek it is clear that the first two uses have the same referent. In Pame the ambiguity was resolved by the use of role terms, thus: "The magistrates were afraid when they heard that the two prisoners were Romans." Similarly in Acts 21:40 the proper name "Paul" is used, which would have sounded awkward in Pame as it had already been used in the previous verse. So a role term, "the prisoner," was substituted.

However, even with apparently obvious role terms, care must be taken as to how they are used. In Nung of Vietnam it is polite to use a role term when referring to oneself or to one's hearer, so it appears frequently in direct quotations. For example, in Genesis 47:30 Jacob asks his son Joseph not to bury him in Egypt but to take his body and bury it in the family burying place. In Nung Jacob refers to himself by the role term "father": "Take father away and bury . . . ." But in Huixteco of Mexico role terms occur in very different situations, and they imply the exclusion of anyone else mentioned in the immediate context. Thus it was not possible to translate literally Acts 9:23, "The Jews plotted to kill him (Saul)" because this would have implied that Saul was not a Jew. Similarly in Acts 18:2, where it says that Paul "found a certain Jew named Aquila," a literal translation would have implied that Paul was non-Jewish. Instead, an inclusive role term using a possessive was substituted, giving "His own people plotted to kill him," and "He found one of his own people called Aquila."

The use of pronouns and demonstratives in tracing participants through a discourse is no less complicated than the use of nouns. Indeed, an unthinking correlation of a pronoun in the RL with one in English or Greek is likely to be extremely misleading, for each language puts its pronouns to very different use. For instance, English may use a pronoun before the noun which refers to the same participant, thus: "Even before she spoke, John knew that the shopgirl was a foreigner." But in Bukidnon Manobo (Philippines) and many other languages, this would be quite impossible. The participant must first be mentioned by a noun, and only thereafter by a pronoun. Or other languages may use pronouns where English does not. In Luke 6:48 the English reads, "He is like a man which built an house" whereas Tampulma (Ghana) prefers "He is like a man who built *his* house," since he was building it for himself.

In Terena (Brazil) there are two third-person pronouns, one referring to a third person to be described later, the other referring to a participant already mentioned. Luke 12:5 contains "Fear him," twice, but it must be translated differently each time, thus "Fear him (the one I'm going to describe) who . . . has power to cast into hell; yea, I say unto you, Fear him (the one I've already mentioned)." Chuj of Guatemala also makes a distinction where English does not: it has two demonstratives meaning roughly "a certain (person)," but one of them means "any single member of the group referred to," while the other means that the speaker has a particular member of the group in mind.

Even when no unexpected contrasts of meanings are involved, pronouns still have characteristic usages in different languages. In Nomatsiguenga the use of a free pronoun in the middle of a discourse (as contrasted with a pronominal affix) often indicates either a new participant, or an old one reappearing from further back than the immediate context. In Shipibo, however, it would have the implication of "the other individual, not the one you logically expect here." In Aguaruna (Peru) also, pronouns are used to show contrast. An entirely different use of the free pronoun is found in Kasem, where every verb, even auxiliary verbs, must have the actor signaled by the appropriate pronoun: thus pronouns are very frequent, and carry no overtones beyond the basic function of identifying the actor.

It cannot even be assumed that a singular form will always refer to a single participant. In Arguaruna there is a pluralizing morpheme in the verb, but it is often omitted, giving an apparently singular form even when the referent is plural. Sometimes the pluralizing morpheme is used when there is a change from a singular subject to a plural one, but once the new subject is established the plural morpheme is no longer used as long as the subject remains the same.

Signaling change of participant

Mention was made earlier of the problem faced in Shipibo of knowing which participant performed which event. Some languages make this easy by always using a noun or an unambiguous pronoun (e.g., a pronoun exhibiting concord) whenever there is a change of agent. Shipibo, on the other hand, signals change of agent mainly by the use of connectives: some connectives mean the same participant is continuing as agent, others mean a change of agent, in which cases complex rules must be applied to find out who the new agent is. Kayapó (Brazil) has a similar system in a simpler form, there being only two connectives involved, one indicating "same agent" and the other "change of agent." The only exception is at paragraph breaks where the "same agent" connective may be used, even if the agent of the preceding clause was different, to signal the same agent as the preceding paragraph viewed as a whole. Cashinawa (Peru) uses connectives with considerable complexity: one suffix means that the participant who was agent in that clause is also agent in the next main transitive clause, even if intransitive clauses or embedded transitive clauses intervene. There are other connectives also which signal same or different agent. Thus John 20:4-7, with several changes of agent, signals this only by connectives: "They went running, he passed Peter, arrived first (same agent follows), bending over saw grave-clothes lying, didn't enter (different agent follows) came behind, entered inside tomb (same agent follows), saw clothes, saw head-wrapping undisturbed by itself."

A point at which special care is needed in signaling participant change is where quoted material is included. Sometimes it is not clear to the reader that the quotation is finished, and that a different participant is now being referred to. One place where such confusion has arisen is Mark 12:18-20, which reads, "[18]Then come unto him the Sadducees, which say there is no resurrection; and they ask him, saying, [19]Master, Moses wrote unto us, If a man's brother die and leave his wife . . . his brother should take his wife, and raise up seed unto his brother. [20]Now there were seven brethren . . . ." In some languages, especially those which do not normally have an overt marker of end-of-quote, it is not immediately obvious that the quotation from Moses concludes at the end of v. 19, and that the Sadducees themselves are telling the story which follows. In Nung (Vietnam) it was necessary to make this clear by adding at the beginning of v. 20, "Then the Sadducee group spoke a story saying . . . ." Without this, readers thought the story also was quoted from Moses.

A similar example is found in Mark 14:27, 28, where Jesus says, "All ye shall be offended because of me this night: for it is written, I will smite the shepherd, and the sheep shall be scattered. But after that I am risen, I will go before you into Galilee." In Chinanteco (Mexico) it was necessary to insert, "Then Jesus said . . ." after the quotation, to make it clear that the quotation had stopped.

COHESION OF EVENTS

It is the function of discourse to convey information about participants (and objects) and events, in other words, to pass on some message about people (or things) and what they did, what was done to them, etc. More abstract types of discourse, which derive their unity from concepts (such as "faith," "higher education," "radioactivity," etc.) rather than from participants, nevertheless exhibit many of the same characteristics. In particular, in every discourse type, it is essential to make the relationship between the events very clear — what event caused what other event, which of two events occurred first, which is an explanation of a whole series of following events, etc. Now, while languages exhibit a wide variety of ways of signaling these relationships, it is also true there are only a limited number of such relationships to be signaled. Hence a knowledge of these relationships may provide a framework, upon which to build a study of the structure of the RL: one may list, for instance, all grammatical constructions found which signal that event A occurred while process B was going on, or that event Z was the purpose of events X and Y.[2] With this knowledge, the translator who faces a verse needing considerable recasting may do so and still keep all the relationships of the original intact. He can see behind the grammar of the original to the events it speaks of, and he can recast these same events in the RL in the most natural way.

Tracing events that are temporally related

The easiest place to start is to study events that are related chronologically. Many discourses are chronologically based; they move along a time-line from the beginning, which is earlier, to the end, which is later, and this time-line forms a unifying thread connecting the whole discourse together. Not all events in the discourse are on the time-line: there will almost always be additional material in the form of quotations, asides, summaries, explanations, etc. But all these, to make sense at all, must be related to a particular part of the time-line.

A common pattern is for events on the time-line to be expressed by predicated verbs, or verbs in main clauses, while material not on the time-line is expressed by dependent verbs or verbs in subordinate clauses. However, this is by no means universal. For instance, Greek uses predicated verbs much less frequently than English: many events which would be expressed in English by a predicated verb are expressed by participles or infinitives, or even abstract nouns, in Greek. Some New Guinea languages, as has been mentioned, have a predicated verb only paragraph-final, while Cashinawa (Peru) goes even further and predicates only the final verb in the discourse — as long as it remains a monologue. Thus we can see that prediction is a grammatical feature which varies con-

[2] These relationships are discussed in detail in chapter 18 of *Translating the Word of God.*

siderably in its significance from language to language: the time-line is better considered, not as those events which are expressed by predication, but as those which are asserted as having taken place, and as having taken place successively. Thus events which are reported out of succession ("She iced the cake *she had baked the day before*"), or which are not asserted as having taken place ("She looked *as if she had seen a ghost*"), are not on the time-line, but are readily relatable to a particular object or event on the time-line.

The time-line and tense

Asserted events, whether they be signaled by predication, tense, mood, or whatever, are always distinguished in some way from events that are not asserted; and languages always have some way of arranging asserted events chronologically, so that the hearer is in no doubt as to their sequence. Beyond that, however, it is not possible to make any universal observations: time-lines seem to appear in a variety of guises throughout the world. The simplest possible case, presumably, would be a language in which each asserted event was mentioned only once, in the order of its actual occurrence. But even here the details are unpredictable; the trans-lator who innocently assumes that the future tense always refers to the future or the past tense to the past is likely very soon to be either considerably confused, or somewhat chastened. In fact he may be unable to find in his language anything which could strictly be called a tense at all, in the traditional Indo-European sense: the chronological factor is signaled in some other way.

In Eastern Otomí (Mexico) the translator, understandably, at-tempted to translate 2 Timothy 3:1-4 ("In the last days perilous times will come . . .") in the future tense. The translation helper, however, soon shifted into past tense. Further study, over a period of time, revealed that in procedural or prophetic discourse it was quite sufficient to use the future tense only at the beginning. Once the correct time-orientation was thus established, past tense was all that was required.

Other discourse-conditioned uses of tense are not uncommon. Bontoc (Philippines) often starts a narrative discourse in the past tense, changes to present tense in the middle of the discourse, and returns to past at the end.

Many languages, including English, orient their tense system to the time of the narration. Thus past tense commonly means, "before the present moment when I'm saying this," and future tense means "after the narration: it still hasn't happened yet as I'm speaking." But in Bahinemo of New Guinea the reference-point to which tenses relate is not the time of the narration; instead, a fresh reference-point is set up for every paragraph. At the beginning of a paragraph a dependent verb establishes an orientation-point: Thereafter the independent verbs throughout the paragraph relate back to the reference-point at the beginning. Thus present tense means "simultaneous with the dependent verb," future tense means "later than dependent verb," and past tense means "prior to dependent verb." A rather similar phenomenon is reported from West Africa, where Kasem has a consecutive tense which is used with either future or past reference — it simply means "this happened next." Thus once past time or future time has been established, consecutive events are reported in consecutive tense, and the use of any other tense implies a break in the time sequence: consecutive tense continues with either future or past reference, until some break in the time sequence occurs. The moral is: study verb tenses with care, and where any unexpected or unexplained tenses occur, check for discourse factors.

Various temporal relationships

Events on the time-line (i.e., excluding summaries, explanations, etc.) are either successive or simultaneous. Successive events, of course, may occur at different intervals of time; some events may follow each other so closely that they almost seem like a single event, whereas in other cases quite a time-lapse may be involved. This may be signaled by tense, particles, connectives or repeated clauses, or it may not be signaled at all unless it carries special significance in the narrative. Often a grammatical construction carries an implicit time-interval with it. In English, if we say, "She made sandwiches and ate them," we usually mean that no long interval elapsed between the making and the eating. The Kasem consecutive tense mentioned above also implies a fairly short time interval: other constructions must be used if there is an appreciable time-lapse. In some languages closely related events have a special construction of their own, more close-knit than regular succession. Mundurukú (Brazil) has such a construction in which the close-knit verbs lack the normal morphemes marking succession, and function as a unit, not allowing any of the interpolations or comments which would be permissible between events in regular succession. Often such close-knit groups form an expected chain of events: given the first verb, the hearer more or less expects the others to follow. Such expected chains might be "Go and get and make," "Get up and go and reach," "Cook food and eat and finish," and so on.

There are also distinctions between different kinds of simultaneous events. Simultaneous events may completely overlap beginning and ending together; they may partially overlap, without matching exactly; or a quick, momentary event may occur within the time-span covered by a process-type event. In Mundurukú, if an event is mentioned twice, and a different event is mentioned in between, then this means the two events were simultanous, and ended together. In Inibaloi (Philippines) there is a construction which can refer to two simultaneous events, or to a process event within which a punctiliar event occurs, or to two events which are really successive, but not significantly so; from the point of view of the narrator they occurred at about the same time. However, many languages would need three different constructions to express these three different patternings of events.

Another event-patterning that needs special care is flashback, that is, a break in the chronological sequence so that after a series of successive events, reference is then made to an event which preceded them in time. Normally such a flashback is used for purposes of identification or explanation, and the original time-line is resumed thereafter. Obviously the translator must know what devices are used for expressing flashback, in what circumstances it is used, how long it may be sustained, and how the return to the time-line is signaled.

Similarly, the time-line is sometimes broken for purposes of flash-forward. For example, in Matthew 27:52-54 there is a sudden switch from the events following immediately upon the death of Christ, to events which happened after his resurrection. Then there is a switch back again to the centurion's reaction at the scene of the crucifixion. In Tampulma, a Ghanian language which normally adheres fairly strictly to a chronological time-line, this was handled satisfactorily by adding the specific time "three days later" to "after his resurrection" in v. 53, and by signaling return to the time-line in v. 54 by the use of a "when" clause with past tense marker. Each language will have its own devices for handling this situation.

More complex time-lines

So far we have assumed the simplest and most straightforward time-line: a steady progression of events, each being mentioned once. But there are many languages which do not present quite such an uncomplicated picture. Ayoré (Bolivia) frequently mentions the same event more than once, i.e., successive verbs refer not to successive events but to the same event. The progression is from the general to the specific, different details being added each time. If the clause giving specific detail is an active one, then it is in turn restated in a clause using the verb "to be." After several verbs have thus been used to recount a single event, the narrative moves on to the next event. In this case, then, the time-line still moves forward unidirectionally, but with pauses at certain events for elaboration.

However, sometimes the time-line is not unidirectional, but may loop back on itself. An incident involving several events is recounted; then the time-line loops back to the beginning of the incident and retells it, usually with more detail. This may happen several times before the story progresses to the next incident. Varying forms of the looped time-line have been reported from South America, New Guinea, and Australia (see especially Grimes and Glock 1970 and Grimes 1972b). Obviously the signals which mark temporal succession and back-looping are different in each case. For example, in Bororo of Brazil temporal sequence is marked throughout an incident; lack of such sequence marking, combined with the fact that pronominalization is held constant, signal a return to the beginning of the incident, which is then retold with varying information and detail. Present evidence suggests that this kind of back-looping normally occurs where the subject matter is of particular significance; obviously it is essential the translator know not only how to signal such a loop in the time-line, but also at what points in the narrative it is appropriate to use it.

Tracing events not temporally related

Obviously one cannot talk of a time-line in discourse types which have little or no chronological orientation: equally obviously, these other types (such as exhortation, description, argument) do exhibit progression. But it is not chronological progression. It therefore makes sense to talk of a theme-line running as a unifying thread through such discourses, just as the time-line runs as a unifying thread through narrative. Certain events will be on the theme-line, others will not be, but will relate to them. Naturally, a theme-line is harder to trace than a time-line: until the overall theme is fairly clear, it may be difficult to decide whether a given event contributes directly to that theme, or only indirectly. Only when the thrust of a whole passage is understood is it possible to assess, for each bit of information, whether it develops the theme, or whether it simply reinforces a point already made without itself moving the theme forward at all.

Thematic material and supporting material will be found to be expressed by typical grammatical constructions and to occur in specific patterns within the paragraph. Those events on the theme-line may either develop the material presented in a topic sentence, or build up gradually to the conclusion presented in a terminator. Often supporting events, not on the theme-line, will strengthen the theme by providing contrasts, comparisons, explanations, alternatives. In fact, these relationships may occur at almost any level: a whole group of events, even a whole paragraph, may present an alternative, a comparison, etc. Every language has its characteristic way of arranging events on the theme-line, and different grammatical constructions are often used with specific significance at certain points in the theme's development. This will be discussed further in chapters 4 and 5. Meanwhile, however, it is necessary to realize that translating the Scriptures involves transferring information from a Greek or Hebrew theme-line to an RL theme-line, i.e., the material, if it is to be understood, should be presented naturally, according to the patterns of the RL theme-line. This may involve presenting the material in a form that looks, on the surface, considerably different from the original — but the purpose is to make the meaning of the original really clear in the RL.

CHANGING THE ORDER OF EVENTS IN THE RL

Reordering of events on the time-line

The Greek time-line in narrative may diverge from strict chronological succession more than many languages. For instance, in Acts 20:11, 12 there is an inversion of chronological order. After Eutychus had fallen to the ground and died, Paul went down and embraced him. Verse 11 then traces Paul's subsequent activities throughout the night, up to his departure the next morning. Verse 12 returns to Eutychus, the fact that he was alive, and that the believers were greatly comforted. In this passage Greek obviously

gives priority to tracing the events that involved the main participant, at the expense of strict chronology. However, in some languages the hearers or readers assume a strictly chronological time-
line, and if vv. 11 and 12 were translated in that order, they would
assume Eutychus was not brought up alive until after Paul's departure.
Hence, to convey the true sequence of events, these verses must be
reordered. In these same verses, the Greek also shows focus on the
main participant in another way. It says in v. 11 "When he therefore had come up again, and had broken bread, and eaten, and
talked a long while . . . ." In fact it is obvious that not only Paul,
but the other believers also, returned upstairs to the meeting room,
broke bread, ate, and talked. Paul would hardly have conducted
these activities by himself, it is simply that the Greek focuses on
him and leaves the others to be understood. In some languages,
this is not possible: if only one person is mentioned, it means that
only one person did it. Thus the Apinayé (Brazil) translation of
these verses has had to change both the time-line and the participant reference here: "They saw that Eutychus was alive again and
were happy. Then they climbed up to the room again and ate.
Then Paul talked to them again until the sun rose. Then he left
them and went away." The same information is conveyed here as
in the original, but it is conveyed in the order which best ensures
its correct interpretation.

The above example involved an inversion in the chronology, but
the events involved were close together in time: two blocks of
events were inverted, but no other material intervened. However,
in the case of flashback other material does intervene. The events
referred to in the flashback may have taken place months or even
years before. In many languages this must be stated very explicitly, otherwise the readers will assume the time-line just carries straight on. Thus in Genesis 44:19 Judah, speaking to Joseph,
says, "My Lord asked his servants, saying, Have ye a father, or a
brother?" The implication is that this question was asked the first
time the brothers visited Egypt; it certainly was not a recent occurrence. Nung of Vietnam, however, has to make the flashback completely explicit, thus: "Previously your servants came; then that
time master asked . . . etc." Otherwise the reader would assume
Joseph had only just made his inquiries.

Greek may also refer to the same event twice, in close succession,
using different verbs. Other languages may do this also, of course:
Ayoré (Bolivia) has already been cited. But some languages cannot

always do this naturally. John 18:10 reads, "Simon Peter having a sword drew it, and smote the high priest's servant, and cut off his right ear." Here the verbs "smote" and "cut off" refer to the same event: there is no suggestion that Peter first hit the servant with the sword and then cut off his ear, the meaning is simply that in striking the blow, Peter cut off Malchus' ear. So in Muong of Vietnam the more general word "smote" is omitted, and the more specific "cut off" is retained. In this way the event is referred to only once, yet the full meaning content is retained.

Reordering of events on the theme-line

Reordering of events is more complex when the discourse is ordered on a theme-line rather than on a time-line, or when time is not the main factor relating the events. In such cases reordering is necessary, not to restore chronological order (where we have the help of experience in doing our reconstructing), but simply because the theme-line patterns of the RL do not match the patterns of the original. In fact, reordering is needed much more frequently in nonchronological material (e.g., the epistles) than in narrative, because most languages stick roughly to a fairly chronological time-line, whereas they differ much more in their theme-line patterns. Usually, translators who have to present complex material in a different order from the Greek do so more or less instinctively, having become accustomed to the way their language presents argument, exhortation, etc. But discourse studies have now reached the point where it should be possible to confirm these hunches by analysis, and to investigate deliberately the way in which a given language presents alternatives, supporting arguments, expansions, hypotheses, thematic assertions, etc.

The examples below illustrate theme-line reordering for a variety of reasons, all of them illustrating theme-line patterns which are of frequent occurrence.

Often events, or groups of events, occur in a paired relationship. Thus one event (or group) may be negative, the other a positive restatement of the same thing. Or one may be generic, the other specific, or one the reason and the other the result. Some languages, including both Greek and English, may use such pairings fairly freely in either order. We may say, "He hates me because I'm honest," or "I'm honest; that's why he hates me." Or, balancing positive and negative, we may say, "I'll be ages yet; I'm not nearly ready," or "I'm not nearly ready, I'll be ages yet." While these may carry a slightly different emphasis, often depending on intonation, either order may be used. However, some languages have a strong preference for one order or the other.

Many languages prefer to put a generic statement before its specific counterpart. Matthew 22:37 and 38 present a pair of statements in the other order, with the more specific first, so Nung (Vietnam) reorders these to read, "This is the greatest and most important commandment: You must love the Lord . . . ." Miahuatlán Zapotec (Mexico) also has a preference for generic preceding specific, and in fact likes to use this construction much more frequently than Greek does, so that many events adequately expressed in Greek by one verb are in Zapotec better expressed by a generic-specific pair. Hence "We ought to give heed" (Heb. 2:1) is translated, "Show we respect to and sit our ear to."

Shipibo (Peru) prefers the order negative-positive when using imperatives. Thus Matthew 19:14 ("Suffer little children, and forbid them not, to come unto me,") has to be inverted to read, "Forbid little children not, to come unto me: permit them to come."

In Greek it was perfectly possible to put the result first, and then the reason leading to the result afterwards. But many languages have a strong preference for putting the result at the end. Thus in Tampulma, a language of Ghana, the order has had to be inverted in Acts 16:38, so that instead of saying, "They (the magistrates) feared when they heard that they were Romans" it now reads, "When the magistrates heard that (Paul and Silas were Romans), fear caught them." This is a fairly brief and simple example of putting a cause before its result. In longer passages, and especially with unfamiliar material, it is particularly important to keep the theme-line clear to the reader, and this is not always easy. In Huixteco (Mexico) for instance, putting the result before the reason first, and then go on to the details and explanations of erable difficulty in translation. Verses 1, 2 and 3a are strong statements about the depth of Paul's sorrow and the truth of his words, and it is not until the end of v. 3 the reader learns the reason for his sorrow, viz., his uncoverted Jewish fellows. Huixteco has to put the reason first, and then go on to the details and explanations of Paul's resulting state. The passage thus starts, "Truly I say it, that much I am sad because my people have not believed." The detailed comments on his sorrow, and on the veracity of his strong claims, then follow, and can be readily understood since the reason has already been stated.

The same chapter affords an example of a different kind of restructuring which was needed in the same language. In vv. 10 to 13 Paul uses the story of God's choosing Jacob before his birth, to prove that God chooses people sovereignly, and not because of their works. But in fact Paul inserts his conclusion into the middle of the story that proves it: the story is carried in vv. 10, 11a, 12, and 13, while the conclusion is found in v. 11b. Huixteco maintains the story as a unity, and then concludes it with the point thus proved. This has the double advantage of preserving the chronological time-line of the story unbroken, and of keeping the proof and the thing proven in the natural Huixteco order.

Apinayé (Brazil) also has a strong preference for putting the reason before the result. Thus Acts 4:34, 35 ("Neither was there any among them that lacked: for as many as were possessors of lands or houses sold them . . ." etc.), is translated by describing the selling of goods and distribution of money first, concluding with the result that there were no believers in need. Hence the passage reads thus: "They used to sometimes sell a building and sometimes sell some land. And take the money from it and give it to the apostles, who would take it and divide it among those who had nothing. Therefore among them there were none who had nothing."

In Greek it is possible to mention at one point a fact which really becomes relevant later: at the later point it is assumed, without necessarily being mentioned again. Not all languages, however, can do this. Once more Apinayé affords an example. Acts 16:1-4 tells how Paul met Timothy at Lystra, and circumcised him to satisfy the Jews, because he wanted him as a traveling companion. That Timothy's father was a Greek is mentioned in v. 1, where Timothy is introduced, but v. 2 switches back to Timothy again. That his father was not a Jew only really becomes relevant in v. 3: "Him would Paul have to go forth with him; (But, implied from v. 1, his father was a Greek, therefore) he took and circumcised him because of the Jews . . . ." Apinayé maintains the unity of vv. 1 and 2 by keeping Timothy in focus throughout, and not mentioning his father until he enters into the argument. Thus vv. 2 and 3 read, "The believers all went around saying Timothy was good. In the cities of Lystra and Iconium they said he was good. Paul arrived and saw him, and wanted to take him along with them. But Timothy was a mixed breed. His mother was an Israel but his father was a non-Israel. Thus Timothy was a mixed breed. Because the Israel ones knew it, Paul circumcised Timothy."

The above example also illustrates a typical configuration of the Apinayé theme-line. The sentence "Timothy was a mixed breed," is followed by the facts of his parentage which illustrate it, and then the original statement is repeated, almost exactly. This is a common Apinayé pattern, particularly when new material is being presented: a statement is made, then details are mentioned, and then the statement is repeated, with or without variations, at the end. This procedure is followed in Acts 4:5, 6, which gives a long list of the officials who gathered together to interrogate Peter and John. First the main proposition is stated: "The next day many of them gathered together. They gathered to hear their talk, in Jerusalem." Then follows the list of officials: elders, scribes, Annas, Caiaphas, etc. And at the end of the list the main proposition is repeated, "Ali of these gathered together."

Naturally, such restructuring is not done indiscriminately, nor is it done solely to make the translation sound more natural. It is done to present the information of the original in the clearest possible way, i.e., in accordance with the patterns normally used in the RL to present that kind of information. When the content is unfamiliar, an unfamiliar presentation such as results from following Greek or Hebrew theme-line patterns makes it much harder for the reader to grasp the message correctly. But in fact, everyone is accustomed to hearing unfamiliar messages in their own language and understanding them with ease, *if they are presented according to familiar usage*. Thus careful adherence to the theme-line patterns of the RL makes it much easier for the reader to grasp unfamiliar material correctly.

CHAPTER 4

Prominence

A story in which every character was equally important and every event equally significant can hardly be imagined. Even the simplest story has at least a central character and a plot, and this means one character is more important than the others, and certain events likewise. Human beings cannot observe events simply as happenings; they observe them as related and significant happenings, and they report them as such.

The New Testament also invests characters and events with different degrees of significance. Sometimes Peter, James, and John hold the attention, while at a different point Judas comes to the fore. Some of Christ's journeys provide simply the linkage between episodes in the narrative, whereas, the triumphal entry into Jerusalem is a journey of very special significance. At a much lower level of discourse structure, a participant may be signaled as of special significance in the discourse by the use of the emphatic pronoun, as in Colossians 1:23 (". . . whereof I (*egō*) Paul am made a minister."). Or an assertion may be made very emphatic by giving the form of a rhetorical question, as in 1 Corinthians 9:1 ("Am I not an apostle? Am I not free?").

Languages have widely differing devices for signaling that one item is of more significance than its neighbors. Though a translator may recognize certain linguistic devices as signaling slight or strong emphasis, he may still have difficulty in knowing when these may be used in the translation, and under what circumstances they sound natural. The problem is intensified by the fact there are no well-accepted discovery procedures or definitions in this area, and that in the matter of terminology every man does what

49

is right in his own eyes. What one investigator calls *focus*, another calls *theme*, and yet another calls *topic*, though the phenomena concerned may be similar in each case. The converse is also true, that two languages may be stated to have *focus* constructions, when in fact the phenomena concerned exhibit virtually no similarities.

The aim of this chapter is to provide the translator with a sort of outline guide, by means of which he can investigate the usage and significance of all types of prominence, and thus more accurately control their use in translation. The term *prominence*, throughout this chapter, refers to any device whatever which gives certain events, participants, or objects more significance than others in the same context. (For this use of the term prominence see Halliday 1969, p. 8, where he says, "I have used the term prominence as a general name for the phenomenon of linguistic highlighting, whereby some feature of the language of a text stands out in some way.") It here covers the entire area for which investigators have used such terms as theme, attention, focus, foreground, figure, topic, and emphasis. Obviously, if one item in a construction is prominent, the others are out of prominence, and these also will require a certain amount of discussion.

Some Initial Considerations: Domain and Signaling Devices

Before discussing different types of prominence in detail, two general matters require consideration, since they apply equally to all types. These are (i) the domain over which the prominence extends, and (ii) the devices by which it is signaled.

Any prominent item is prominent within a certain domain. This is different from simply saying where the prominence signals occur, whether within the verb phrase, clause-initial, paragraph-final, or whatever. Every prominence signal occurs within some clause, or perhaps preposed to it: but it can have a significance that extends considerably beyond the clause in which it occurs. The investigator must ask himself, within what area does this item have special significance? *What is its domain?*

Thus Cromack says for Cashinawa (1968, p. 309), "The first word in the text body is highlighted as the topic in primary focus for a paragraph or series of paragraphs until another focused item, probably already expressed in the discourse introduction, is picked up in the narration." In this case the first word may stand alone, not strictly part of any clause — that is its physical location. The *extent* of the significance of this first word is made clear in the quotation:

its domain covers "a paragraph or series of paragraphs until another focused item . . . is picked up . . . ."

Sometimes, however, the domain of prominence extends no further than the clause in which it occurs. Thus in the same language (*ibid.*, p. 326) particles indicating slight or strong emphasis or insistence occur commonly with commands, permissive questions, and statements. Their domain extends no further than the command or question concerned, as in Genesis 2:16, which reads, "To him the Lord God commanded, 'These different garden trees, their fruit you may *certainly* eat.' "

Unfortunately for the translator, the devices by which prominence is signaled are legion, and even within one language several different devices may be used simultaneously, with a different significance in each case. Repetition, use of particles and affixes, special tone patterns, unusual order of words, intensifying verbs or tenses of verbs — these are just some of the devices used to signal prominence, and a translation which lacks them will sound flat and foreign. A degree of order may be brought to the confusion, however, when it is realized that these various signaling devices may be used in one of two different ways. Sometimes, in a given grammatical unit, some element must be prominent, and the narrator or translator has to choose which one. Within each clause, or each sentence, or each paragraph, a choice has to be made; an item has to be selected for prominence. In this case, there is often an expectation that a certain item will be chosen; there is a norm. Thus in Bororo (Brazil) (Crowell, 1973, p. 10) the initial element in a clause is the theme of that clause, and this position is usually occupied by the subject. When expectation is thus fulfilled, and the anticipated item is given prominence, then the degree of intensity is very slight. It is still true to say that, in Bororo clause structure, initial position signals prominence, in this case thematic prominence; but when the expected norm in fact occurs, the degree of prominence is small. However, if some unexpected element is given thematic position, then the intensity of prominence is much greater.

The other way of using prominence devices is by adding them to constructions which do not necessarily carry prominence at all, in their normal use. Here one is not constantly making a choice as to whether to make something prominent or not. Normally, there is no particular prominence, but when the occasion demands it there is a device available in the language for providing it. Such extrasystemic devices normally give rise to a prominence that is fairly strong in intensity.

The Significance of Prominence in the Discourse

It will be maintained here that, in spite of the many terms now current for different kinds of prominence, and in spite of the innumerable overt forms taken by prominence features, there are nevertheless only three main values of prominence in discourse, and that all the different varieties and subvarieties of prominence in different languages occur with one or the other of these three values. Those values will here be called *theme, focus,* and *emphasis,* and each will be defined and described in turn. Notice that prominence values imply no particular correlation with any particular type of signal or combination of signals. It is not the nature of the signal, but the value that is signaled, that concerns us.

Prominence that occurs with *thematic* significance is, in effect, saying to the hearer, "This is what I'm talking about." Such information is prominent in the discourse because it carries the discourse forward, it contributes to the progression of the narrative or argument. It contrasts with nonthematic material, which rather serves as a commentary on the thematic, but does not in itself contribute directly to the progression of the theme. The theme-line or time-line (which are variant forms of thematic material) extend throughout the body of the discourse.

Prominence that occurs with *focus* significance is saying to the hearer, "This is important, listen." It picks out items of thematic material as being of particular interest or significance. Different items may be picked out for focus at different points along the theme-line: the domain of focus varies from language to language, but is rarely longer than two or three paragraphs, sometimes much shorter.

Prominence that occurs with *emphatic* significance normally involves the speaker-hearer relationship in some way. It says to the hearer either "You didn't expect that, did you?", or "Now, I feel strongly about this." In other words, emphasis has two different functions: it highlights an item of information which the narrator considers will be surprising to the hearer, or else it warns the hearer that the emotions of the speaker are quite strongly involved. Both functions tend to operate over a relatively short domain, to have typical intonation patterns as part of the signal, and to be extrasystemic in structure; hence they are treated here as variant forms of the same basic value.

In distinguishing the different values of prominence it is perhaps helpful to consider the total discourse as analogous to a theatrical production. The theme is the unfolding plot, always seen against its background of minor characters and stage properties. Focus is the spotlight, which may be playing continuously, or switched on and off as appropriate. Emphasis is the clash of cymbals or some similar climax in the accompanying music. Unfortunately, in real languages the three are not always so easy to distinguish, owing to the complex nature of the signals involved and their relationship with the grammar. Nevertheless, the analogy provides a useful guide in trying to assess the value of prominence in any given case.

PROMINENCE WITH THEMATIC VALUE

Thematic material is material that develops the theme of a discourse, by contrast with background material, which fills out the theme but does not develop it. The theme of a discourse constitutes a progression, called in chapter 3 the time-line and the theme-line; here cohesion and prominence meet in one construction, or rather, set of constructions. Inasmuch as it constitutes a progression, the theme-line signals cohesion; inasmuch as it contrasts with background material, it signals prominence, of the type here called theme, though elsewhere it goes under various other names such as figure, foreground, focus, primary content, etc.

The concept of the theme-line, by whatever term it is designated, has proved to be a helpful one to translators, especially in the area of selecting the most appropriate construction to convey a given kind of information. It must not be thought, however, that widespread usefulness implies widespread agreement, in detail, on the nature of the theme vs. background contrast, for such agreement does not exist. Rather, each investigator tends to adopt simply the bare contrast as such, and apply it as best fits the language concerned. It is not surprising if languages, which differ from each other at almost every point, differ also in their theme-and-ground configurations. It is because languages differ so much that linguistic tools need to be flexible, and from the translator's point of view, the more flexible the theme-line concept remains, the better. Translators requiring a practical approach which is at the same time more sophisticated than the one suggested here, should consult Grimes, "The Thread of Discourse," pp. 103-124.

Theme and background: varied approaches

The theme-background contrast has been applied to the broad sweep of discourse, and to its minutest detail. Samplings will be given here of different approaches. They all have in common that certain material is considered as foreground, as against other material that is background; but the material thus envisaged ranges from single events to whole paragraphs.

The theme-background concept was introduced into current linguistic description by Taber (1966), using the terms "figure" and "ground." He says (pp. 84-85), "one finds . . . a fundamental dichotomy cutting across the object and event terms . . . . Certain objects constitute part of the figure: these are the major participants, who occur as subjects of the events of the narrative and whose actions move the story along. In contrast to these there are other objects (often inanimate, but not always) which constitute part of the ground. Typically they are introduced . . . as part of the motivation or as part of the scene . . . , and during the course of the story they are mentioned either in dialogue or in the form of circumstantial complements . . . .

"Similarly, certain events . . . constitute the progression of the story; these are figure events. In contrast, there are other events . . . which constitute part of the ground, since they do not advance the story but characterize the background against which the story evolves. Ground events frequently occur in clauses embedded in noun phrases, or without a predicator . . . ."

Two points deserve special note. (1) The terms "figure" and "ground" are applied to events and things, not to large stretches of discourse. (2) Certain hints are given as to the grammatical forms in which these things or events are expressed in the language. From the translator's point of view, this is of crucial importance. There would be no point in viewing a discourse as a theme against a background, if this constituted an end in itself. Rather, theme and background have their own distinctive expressions in the grammar, and a translation may be cumbersome and hard to follow if these are confused. Hence the translator uses a theme-background contrast in his analysis so that he may convey each type of information by means of the appropriate construction in his translation.

Other languages have been analyzed with theme and background applying not to things and events as such, but to larger stretches of discourse. Thus in Kasem a proposition as a whole is considered as thematic or nonthematic, rather than any one thing or event in it. This correlates with a grammatical structure in which only one event is asserted in each clause: a clause or sometimes a clause series with one main verb, is the grammatical counterpart of a proposition, and different clause types convey thematic and nonthematic material. However, such an analysis would be quite

unsuitable for a language like Greek, which frequently expresses
several propositions in one clause. In this case, it seems prima facie
probable that a single clause may carry both thematic and background material, appropriately expressed; hence a unit smaller than
the clause (though possibly still expressing a single proposition)
would be the grammatical vehicle of the theme-background contrast.

Sheffler uses the terms "primary content" and "secondary content"
to describe the theme-background patterns of Munduruku. These
terms are applied to stretches of discourse at least one clause in
length, often longer. They are described in terms of the kind of
message they convey. She says (1970, p. 1), "Primary content
reports the progress of specific agents toward stated targets or goals,
and the impeding or promoting of that progress by other participants." She also says (p. 3), "Secondary content consists of descriptions, explanations, conclusions, and summaries of primary events
and the included participants. It provides the background against
which the narrative is told." Primary content is described in terms
of events on an event-line referred to by finite verbs, together with
their relators. The various types of secondary content are described
in detail, being distinguishable from primary content in their structure, distribution, and system of participant reference. Here again,
then, we see that thematic and nonthematic material have different
expressions in the grammar.

Kayapó (Brazil) distinguishes different types of paragraph on a
thematic basis. "Base paragraphs" carry the story forward. Transition and explanatory paragraphs either repeat known information,
or provide nonevent information such as identification, description,
nonactualized events, etc. Though the thematic contrast is here
expressed in high-level grammatical units, it is nevertheless obviously the same contrast that has been observed elsewhere, between
foreground and background material.

Identifying theme and background in nonnarrative discourse

Most of the examples quoted in the preceding section were based
on the analysis of narrative discourses. Since narrative develops
along a chronological theme-line (i.e., a time-line), it is usually
not too difficult to decide whether a given clause (or other selected
unit) conveys thematic or background information. If it reports an
event in the event-series, occurring in chronological sequence, it is
thematic; if it reports anything else, it is background. The distinction is not so easy to apply, however, to nonnarrative discourses.

These develop along a theme-line, which may be argumentative, hortatory, or explanatory; material which might have a background function in narrative may be thematic in these other types of discourse. Contrastive material, for example, would normally be in the background in narrative, but might well be on the theme-line in argumentative discourse, where the argument sometimes develops by means of contrasts. It may be helpful, therefore, to consider further the type of material that may be encountered in theme and background, with special reference to nonnarrative discourse.

The easiest point of departure is probably to discuss some definitions that have been given of background material. Though these were based on narrative discourse, the transfer to other discourse types is made more readily than with thematic material. Grimes and Glock (1970, pp. 420, 421) state, "Collateral information . . . sets off events against alternative possibilities that do not form part of the main event sequence . . . . Background information is . . . either general information that is independent of time; or else refers to events that take place outside the event sequence, but that relate to it in some way. In either case it may be deleted without disturbing the rest of the narrative, or it can be expressed at any one of a number of points without affecting anything else." The final sentence quoted provides us with a valuable criterion for detecting background material in any kind of discourse: if it may be removed or transferred without disrupting the development of the discourse, then it is part of the background.

Stout and Thomson (1971, p. 252) quote a somewhat similar list: ". . . that which identifies characters, that which describes settings, that which speaks of alternative possibilities that do not actually happen or which gives the narrator's personal ideas or experiences . . . and that which gives general knowledge that is time-independent or that concern events that are not part of the narrative."

Secondary content in Mundurukú was earlier described as consisting of "comments, parentheses, flashbacks, and summaries." Further detail here reveals that background material in Mundurukú includes description, contrast, parenthesis giving setting or manner of an event, explanation from a viewpoint not that of the main actor, causal or contrastive summaries. These could be applied to nonnarrative material with little or no adaptation.

Tracing the theme-line in nonnarrative material is less straightforward because of the variety of material involved, even within one discourse. The best practical approach is to work a paragraph at a time, while keeping the total discourse in mind, and to assess for each paragraph the main thrust of its argument. Often the topic sentence or the terminator will supply a clue to this, or even a complete summary. The topic sentence may state the relationship of the paragraph to the one before, or may link the paragraph to some other point earlier in the discourse, or may indicate the value of the paragraph within the discourse as a whole, whether illustrative, developmental, marking a turning point, etc. All these are valuable clues to the nature of the paragraph. (For further detail on paragraph structure, see Lord, 1964, Longacre, 1968.)

The nucleus of the paragraph will develop the theme either sequentially, or by means of such relationships as reason-result, cause-effect, comparison or contrast between two items, parallelism, coordination, contradiction, explanation, plan and execution, alternatives, question and answer, etc. Once the overall development of the paragraph is clear, material considered as probably background in function may be tested as mentioned earlier, by whether or not it can be omitted, and by comparison with known types of background material. Grammatical features already known to be indicative of thematic or background material in the language provide evidence which is often decisive.

An outline of procedure for tracing theme-line in nonnarrative discourse might be as follows:

1. Review total argument of discourse.
2. Isolate paragraph for consideration; assess its contribution to the total argument, using clues provided in the topic sentence or in the body of the paragraph.
3. Mark all material known to be thematic or background by unambiguous grammatical signals.
4. Mark all material clearly thematic or nonthematic by its content, or by other clues such as intonation.
5. Test remaining doubtful material by omitting it, and by trying to assess its contribution to the argument.
6. Keep a note of unanalyzed residues, in case a later paragraph provides unambiguous parallels.

Theme at clause level

It was stated earlier that prominence is always operative within a certain domain; Bororo was cited as having the thematic element of its clause in initial position. All our later discussion of theme, however, has been concerned with higher levels of the discourse, and "theme" has been taken to mean, "what I am talking about in this discourse." Is it possible for a clause to have a theme of its own, and if so, in what sense?

First, of course, this point must be made clear: if a clause has a theme of its own, this does not cancel out any contribution which that clause makes to the theme-background configuration of the discourse as a whole. The two operate at different levels. Secondly, it may be said categorically that clause-level theme is well-established for a few languages; it remains for further research to show how widely this applies, and how it helps the translator.

The concept of theme within the clause was developed for English by Halliday (1967 and 1968) and has been taken up by others. The theme is that element which states what is being talked about in the clause, providing it with a point of departure: the remainder of the clause Halliday terms the rheme, i.e., what is being said about the theme. So a clause divides into what is being talked about, and what is being said about it.

It may readily be seen that "what is being talked about," is exactly what the term *theme* has been taken to mean throughout this chapter. Within the clause, however, theme does not contrast with background, as in discourse, but with rheme. It is the jump-off point, and not necessarily the most prominent item, in the clause which forms its domain. Where that jump-off point, i.e., the topic which the rest of the clause is talking about, is exactly what would have been expected from the preceding discourse, then of course it carries no prominence at all. This would occur, for instance, where a subject pronoun occurred first in thematic position, but referred to exactly the same participant who had been repeatedly referred to as subject throughout the paragraph. It may still be true that that participant is highly prominent in said paragraph or series of paragraphs, but the word which refers to him is not the prominent word in that particular clause. Thus while theme at discourse level always carries a degree of prominence, theme at clause level is somewhat different; it carries no prominence whatever if it is expected. However, it does have another very useful function: it signals the point at which the information carried by the clause attaches to the preceding discourse; it provides cohesion. Thus before the information is given, the hearer is already alerted as to where it will fit in to what he already knows.

If, on the other hand, the item functioning as theme is not the expected item, then in this case theme carries considerable prominence. So far, studies on clause-level theme have all come from languages with flexible word order. A given position, usually initial, is thematic, and the order of the words may be changed to make the desired element the theme. In languages where word order is variable, therefore, the theme-rheme contrast may well provide the needed clue to explain apparently random variations.

Bacairi (Brazil) is of interest because in its pronoun system, certain third-person forms are thematic and others nonthematic. Word order is also flexible, the first element in the clause normally being the theme. But since theme may be signaled simply by the selection of a third-person pronoun, it is possible to place the pronoun later in the clause and leave the first position vacant for some other item. In this case the item selected for first position is the one that carries new information, which is thus put into prominence.

Levinsohn (in a private communication) reports a device used in Inga (Colombia) whereby a previously-mentioned participant may be shown to have further significance in the story by the use of an optional suffix. Thus Mark 2:14b reads "Levi-suffix rising-up followed him." Levi has been previously mentioned in the same verse, and it would have been quite possible to leave the second mention as nonprominent (expected) theme. But since he has further significance in the following narrative, when Jesus went to his house, it is better here to mark the second mention with the suffix, so that his prospective prominence is recognized.

Both Bacairi and Inga are languages with highly flexible word-order, but which also have other devices available for signaling the thematic elements in the clause. It remains to be seen whether languages with invariant word order may provide a variety of such alternative ways of signaling the theme-rheme contrast.

Theme in translation

It is obviously important in translation that material which is thematic in the original should be translated by appropriate thematic constructions in the RL. Analysis of Greek discourse structure is not far enough advanced to allow a detailed study at this stage, but enough is known to illustrate the problem. The Greek relative clause has a wide variety of functions: one of these is thematic, that is to say, it carries information that is on the theme-line. An example of this is found in Colossians 1:12, 13, "Giving thanks unto the Father, *which* hath made us meet . . . *who hath* delivered us . . . ." In this case the relative pronoun, normally translated by English *who, which,* does not carry any backgrounding significance whatever, it simply serves as a participant-referent for the clause, and is then better translated by *he, it,* or the appropriate personal pronoun. In many languages, including English, the relative construction has a backgrounding effect: it either describes or identifies the participant concerned, but at the same time the descriptive or identifying information is signaled as being off the theme-line. If a Greek relative clause is translated by an RL relative clause in such cases, the effect is that a quantity of information which should be in the foreground is stated in a background construction, to the confusion of the reader. Often the reader "pigeonholes" such information in his mind, and presses on trying to get back to the theme again, not realizing that the material he has thus pushed into the background is, in fact, the theme he is looking for. In translation, therefore, a Greek theme-line construction should be translated by an RL theme-line construction, and similarly with background materials.

An example of how this works out in practice is provided by the translation of 1 Peter 1:17 into Kekchi (Guatemala). That verse reads, "If ye call on the Father, who without respect of persons judgeth according to every man's work, pass the time of your sojourning here in fear." In this verse, the "if" does not cast any doubt on whether they called on the Father — Peter knew they did. And the relative clause does not give background detail on the Father's character, but rather a reason for the readers to behave with fear. Hence both these constructions are translated by main clauses in Kekchi, thus, "God judges each person according to what he does, and He does not show favoritism. 'Our Father' you say, when you pray. If that is what you say, may you have fear in your hearts as long as you are here in this world."

PROMINENCE WITH FOCUS VALUE

Focus is that type of prominence which acts as a spotlight, playing on the thematic material to bring some of it especially to the attention. In some languages, focus is an obligatory category and one cannot avoid using it: at any point, some clause or participant or event must be in focus. In other languages there is no such all pervasive system of spotlighting, but devices are available whereby attention may be drawn to particular elements as desired. In Vagla (Ghana) there are two sets of tone perturbation patterns operative throughout an entire clause, and every clause must carry one set of patterns or the other: it is an obligatory system. Normally one set is used in all main clauses in conversation, the other in main clauses in narrative, but the occurrence of a conversation-type tone pattern on a narrative clause will draw special attention to it. In other languages, focus is not upon a clause as such but on some element in the clause — on a participant, location, or whatever is relevant at the time.

One language which has an obligatory system of focus on participants is Bacairi. Here, focus on the major participant is obligatory and only one participant may be in focus in a given paragraph or episode. In Bacairi this is signaled by the pronominal system: one of the third-person pronouns is both focal and thematic, and it is used, "to introduce the main character. (It) is also used for any new character who is placed in focus later" (Wheatley, 1973, pp. 106-07). It is possible for other characters to figure as agents while the first character is still in focus, but they are then referred to as nonfocal agents; only one character is in focus at any one time in Bacairi narrative. Participants may also be distinguished as being in or out of focus by using different forms of nominalized verbs to refer to them.

An example of how this works out in translation may be seen in John 1. Jesus is the focal character, and is referred to by the focal and thematic pronoun. Verse 3 ("all things were made by him,") has to be changed to the focal form of the nominalized verb so as to maintain Jesus as focal character, so it reads, "He was *the maker* (focal form) of all things." When John the Baptist is introduced in verse 6 a nonfocal pronoun is used, and in verse 7 ("the same came for a witness") the nominalized form of the verb "to come" ('the-one-who-came') is the nonfocal form.

Bacairi also provides some interesting material related to the domain of focus. "Another aspect of focus is that it has to be renewed periodically . . . . It is as though main focus status were like a static electrical charge that leaks away into the atmosphere unless reestablished" (Wheatley, 1973, p. 28). Thus after a certain number of clauses, (varying from two to about twenty according to the amount of secondary material present), the focal character may be once more referred to by a nonfocal pronoun. At this point it is possible either to continue for a time without any character being in overt focus, or to renew the focus on the original focal character by using either the focal pronoun or a proper name. The application of these focus patterns to New Testament translation will obviously require considerable sensitivity to a variety of factors affecting prominence and domain.

Unlike Bacairi, which can have participants functioning as agents while still marked as out-of-focus, many languages assume that the participant functioning as agent is in focus, and that this is expressed grammatically as the subject of a clause. This creates considerable problems in translation, since Greek could have several different participants all featuring as agents (and sometimes all as grammatical subjects) in the space of one verse. A literal translation here would cause the readers considerable confusion as focus was apparently shifted rapidly from character to character. In Cakchiquel (Guatemala) it is natural to keep one participant in focus for several clauses, and therefore verses sound extremely unnatural if they switch focus from one participant to another and then back to the first again. In these cases Cakchiquel sometimes uses a passive construction so as to maintain focus on the first participant throughout. An example of this is found in Mark 9:31, "The Son of man is delivered into the hands of men, and they shall kill him." Here the Cakchiquel reads, "I the Son of man will be delivered into the hands of men and *I will be killed*," thus avoiding introducing "they" as grammatical subject of "will kill." Similarly Mark 16:9 ("he appeared first to Mary Magdalene, out of whom he had cast seven devils,") is changed to read "he appeared first to Mary Magdalene, *out of whom were cast seven devils by Jesus.*" This avoids using the name "Jesus" as grammatical subject once Mary Magdalene has been introduced, as she is to be the subject in the following verse also.

Mezquital Otomí (Mexico) is another language which makes full use of focus, although it does not constitute an obligatory category in the language. In this case it is frequently a particularly significant element which is put into prominence within the paragraph. Wallis (1971, p. 19) says, "Within the paragraph, a whole sentence may have focus function. A *rhetorical interrogative* sentence reinforces a proposition already stated or implied. A *paraphrase sentence* is a common focus device . . . ." Otomí also signals focus within the sentence, usually by means of front-shifting the prominent element. Sometimes, however, an element that is normally peripheral in the sentence acquires significance at discourse level, and in this case devices other than front-shifting can be brought into play. Thus Matthew 2:13-15, has a strong locational focus: Joseph is told to escape to Egypt, does so, and remains there. This focus on a specific location is brought out in Otomí not by front-shifting but by repeated locative references. Thus the sentence, "be thou there until I bring thee word" (v. 13), carries three overt expressions of location in Otomí: an anaphoric locative, a locative aspect in the verb prefix, and a postclitic which stands for the adverb "there." "Such locative redundancy . . . is common and natural in Otomí narratives where location is crucial to the plot" (Wallis, 1971, p. 20).

Sometimes a construction which normally signals theme ("this is what I'm talking about") can be used in an unexpected way so as to bring certain information into focus. In Oksapmin (New Guinea) independent verbs normally occur in sentence-final position. Any nonevent information occurring sentence-final, therefore, is unexpected, and carries significance within the discourse; it is in focus. This device has been used in the translation of Genesis 22:8, 9, where one sentence ends not with an event but with a location, "the place where God had told him." This brings the location into prominence, which would be natural for Oksapmin, since several important events take place there.

Inga (Colombia) has two ways of putting a new element into focus in the sentence. It may come either at the end, in which case the verb preceding it carries the aspect marker, or it may precede the verb, in which case the focused item carries the aspect marker. Thus Matthew 7:24 (". . . a wise man which built his house upon a rock,") can be translated either as "wise-man house-built-aspect *on-stones*" or as "wise-man *on-stones-aspect* house-built." Both translations give the correct focus, i.e., upon the place where the man wisely chose to build. An included clause may also be focused on in the same way, thus: "to-hill he-went-aspect *with-God to-speak.*" (Mark 6:4b.)

PROMINENCE WITH EMPHATIC VALUE

Emphasis, the kind of prominence which provides the discourse with speaker-hearer factors involving emotion or expectation, has not usually caused translators the kind of problem found under focus. Nevertheless, in this area also, there is evidence that in some languages much greater naturalness could be achieved by the use of emphasis, and on occasion wrong meaning could be conveyed by its misuse.

Devices for providing emphasis are normally particles, word-order (especially front-shifting) and repetition, but of course there are other possibilities. Ayoré (Bolivia) uses repetition, thus "no they kill us, no they kill us" is not simply a statement of fact, but carries the strong implication that "we were sure they were going to kill us but (relief!) they didn't." Cubit and Clayre (1970) report for Kayan (Borneo) that in a particular sentence type two particles occur, one of which signals "this information is important," while the other signals, "this information is incidental, not unduly significant."

Vagla (Ghana) has several devices for emphasis as distinct from the tone-perturbation focus mentioned earlier. In Matthew 7:21 two sets of people are contrasted: "Not everyone that saith unto me, Lord, Lord, shall enter into the kingdom of heaven; but he that doeth the will of my Father . . . ." In Vagla this reads, "Those who call me Master, Master, *they all not-emphatic fut-emphatic* will enter God's kingdom. The person who is doing my Father's will *he-emphatic will-emphatic* enter God's kingdom." Thus not only emphatic pronouns, but emphatic negative and future particles, are used to emphasize the contrast, which was an unexpected one to the hearers. The same language has a completely different device for emphasis when it is not the subject of the sentence that is emphasized. Thus in Matthew 9:34 ("He casteth out devils through the prince of devils") the Vagla reads, "Through the insides-power of the prince of bad spirits, he is able to chase bad spirits," and vowel-lengthening is used on the word "insides" (which comes at the end of the phrase in Vagla) to put emphasis on the whole preceding phrase.

Sometimes with cases of reported speech the translator does not realize that emphasis is involved because of the way the content is stated in the Greek (or English) text. This applies particularly when an indirect quotation is made, and the emotion involved is stated outside the quotation itself. Thus in Acts 10:45 we read, "they . . . were astonished . . . because that on the Gentiles also was poured out the gift of the Holy Ghost." The mere statement that the Gentiles had received the Holy Ghost is not in itself emphatic; the fact that emotion and emphasis were present is shown in the reporting verb "astonished." In Halang (Vietnam) the concept of "amazed" or "astonished" is difficult to express. There is no equivalent reporting verb. Yet simply to translate "the believers said, the Holy Spirit has been poured out on the Gentiles too" would obviously be flat, and dynamically not faithful to the original. The problem was solved by the use of a rhetorical question to express surprise, thus: "The believers said, 'Why did the Holy

Spirit fall on non-Jews . . . ?'" Other languages have to do this even more widely, to express such concepts as "accuse," "rebuke," "command," etc. In other words, speaker-hearer relationship has to be expressed in direct speech, not in the narrative context. (See examples in Auca and Navajo, NOT 10.)

Frequently in the gospels the Lord emphasizes something important by saying, "I say unto you," (Luke 16:9 et al.) or "Verily, verily, I say unto you." It is essential for the translator to realize that these statements are primarily prominence-statements, not content-statements. That is, the Lord was not informing them that He was speaking to them, of which they were well aware; He was drawing attention to some particular element in His teaching. Such expressions were part of the speaker-hearer relationship. A literal translation here may sound very clumsy or misleading. Kasem (Ghana) has two ways of translating "I say unto you." One simply means "I am talking to you," which is a statement of the obvious; the other is used when a statement has previously been made, and misunderstood by the hearer, so the speaker is patiently going over the whole thing again. Obviously neither of these is a suitable translation in the context of the Lord's teaching. In many cases some much better translation may be found in a teacher-pupil context — "Now, all be hearing me," "Listen well to this," etc. A literal translation of "Verily, verily" is possible. "Truth," followed by an emphatic particle, is quite a common phrase, but it is most frequently used when someone has been accused of telling lies and is emphatically denying it. Again, this hardly fits the context of the Lord's teaching.

PROBLEMS CONNECTED WITH THE ANALYSIS OF PROMINENCE

Earlier in this chapter it was pointed out that there has been considerable confusion concerning terminology in the whole area of prominence. This was an understatement. The whole subject, not simply its terminology, has been an area in which translators have been singularly unsure of their footing, and this uncertainty has reflected itself in their translations. It is possible that unnaturalness has been greater in this area than any other.

Since languages differ so widely in their use of prominence, it is not possible to present any solution to this problem here. However, it is hoped that an analysis of the factors which have hitherto caused confusion would enable a translator to find his way through the prominence features of his particular RL with somewhat surer footsteps. The "confusion factors" will be considered in turn.

Grammatical versus functional definitions

One fact will have been obvious throughout this chapter: there has been a certain correlation between the three types of prominence posited, and the grammatical domains and signaling devices correlated with them. Theme, which carries the message forward, has the whole discourse as its domain, and specific clause types as its signaling devices. Focus, which spotlights certain elements in the theme, may be obligatory (hence part of a system) or optional (nonsystemic), and is shorter in domain than theme. Emphasis, which is the most intense type of prominence, is always nonsystemic — hence in languages where focus also is nonsystemic (as exemplified in the quotations from Otomí earlier in this chapter) there may be no difference between the two, other than intensity — or they may not be distinguishable at all.

Sometimes it is possible to give unambiguous grammatical definitions of different types of prominence. For Melanau (Malaysia) Iain Clayre is able to say that focus is a characteristic property of the nucleus of the clause, affecting the form of the verb, and determining the word order. Emphasis determines word order in the periphery of the clause, and occasionally in the nucleus, but never affects the form of the verb.

For many other languages, however, no such clear picture emerges — a particle which signals emphasis in one construction may be entirely without prominence in another. In other words, grammatical and functional criteria clash. The danger here is that the translator will label a particular construction as "focus" or "emphasis" in his mind, and then use it as such in all circumstances. The translator must constantly bear in mind that a grammatical signal may have varying functions. He must investigate both the signals and the functions separately. Vagla was mentioned earlier as an example of a language which could put focus on a main clause in narrative by the use of certain tone-perturbation patterns. Yet those identical patterns are also used to signal flashback (which is normally considered to be background rather than thematic material), and in other constructions carry no prominence at all; they are just obligatory to that construction. This may be highly confusing to handle, but it illustrates the point that languages are simply not as neat and tidy as the investigator would like them to be, and that prominence signals and prominence values must be carefully distinguished.

Signals with double function

Sometimes a certain grammatical signal, for example a pronoun or a particle, may signal two or more factors simultaneously. The danger here is of recognizing one of its uses and failing to realize the existence of the other. An example of such double function is found in Bacairi (already mentioned earlier in the chapter). Certain pronouns in Bacairi signal "third person animate, previously referred to": in other words, they function as part of the cohesion system. The same pronouns also function in the prominence system, however. It would be a serious mistake, for example, to use the pronoun *maca* whenever such a third person referent was required, regardless of whether it was thematic or not; a different pronoun is available for nonthematic third person reference. In all such examples of double function, the danger is of recognizing one function and ignoring the other. If the translator finds himself saying, "I can't think *why* they sometimes use x and sometimes use y; they both seem to mean the same," then he should be aware of the possibility of a signal functioning in two systems at once.

Marked and unmarked value of prominence signals

As was mentioned in the focus section, very often prominence is signaled in some systematic way. It may be that the last word in the clause is the prominent one, or the first word, or the stressed word, or the word marked by a certain particle: the kind of signal is immaterial, what matters is that in every clause some item carries this signal. What is not so often realized is that usually there is a high expectation that one particular item will be so marked — that the last word will be the verb, that the agent will be marked by the particle, etc. And where it is the expected item that occurs with the prominence signal, then the degree of prominence is slight or non-existent. This "unmarked" form, though it carries the outward signal of prominence, is not in fact very prominent. But if an unexpected item is put in the prominent position, then attention is immediately drawn to it: it is the marked form.

An outstanding example of this is provided by many Philippine and related languages. There is by now an extensive literature on this subject (see Reid 1966, Miller 1964, Elkins 1970, Ward and Forster 1967, etc.) much of which would not be relevant in other areas of the world. But a simplified account of the general characteristics of the system may prove useful here. In such languages, one of the nominal elements carries a focus marker. This marker does not show whether the nominal concerned is the agent of the verb, the goal of the verb, or in any other relationship to the verb: it simply marks this nominal as the topic (many other terms have been used) of the clause. It is an affix on the verb which shows the role relationship in which the topic noun stands: different affixes signal "the topic noun is subject," "the topic noun is goal," etc. Two extreme interpretations of this are possible: (i) every clause obligatorily has some item prominent; (ii) it is a purely grammatical feature, a rather unusual way of signaling role relationships within the clause. In fact, neither of these two extremes seems to present the true picture by itself: the marking of a particular nominal as topic always has grammatical significance, and in addition it has *either marked or unmarked* prominence. In other words, given certain circumstances, it is expected that a certain nominal (subject, instrument) will be the topic. This is the unmarked occurrence, since it has grammatical significance but almost no prominence value. Abrams reports for Bilaan (1961, pp. 391-402) that this correlates with verb classes: each verb carries a focus-expectation, and it is only marked for a focus contrary to that expectation. This seems akin to the situation reported by Beatrice Clayre for Dusun (Borneo) that in that language the objective focus seems to be unmarked, i.e., it is the normal and expected form.

However, widespread agreement that the marking of a nominal as topic has grammatical significance, and frequently carries unmarked focus, does not solve the translator's problem of when to use the marked focus, i.e., when to mark as topic an unexpected item. Ward and Forster (1967, p. 41) suggest that "the topic appears to be related primarily to something other than the predicate of an individual clause, perhaps to some as yet unanalyzed unit of discourse." Clayre, working from a Dibabawon text provided by Forster, suggests that a participant may be put into focus by repeated use of subject focus, then drop back into object focus, maintained even though a new participant enters. This new participant may later be given prominence by the use of subject or referent focus followed by object focus as before. Thus it would seem possible to divide the text into stretches, the main participant in each being singled out by nonobject focus at the beginning of the stretch but not thereafter.

If this is borne out by research in related languages, then the translator will find the use of marked focus a powerful tool in providing cohesion and tracing participants through discourse. And once more a single signal turns out to be of multiple significance, providing grouping, cohesion and prominence within the discourse.

CHAPTER 5

Information

INFORMATION RATE

Introduction

The task of the translator is to communicate information. Specifically, his task is to communicate the same information as is conveyed by the original, but using those forms which are appropriate to that kind of information in the RL. The previous chapters studied in some detail the forms of presentation appropriate to information involving participants and events, with the varying degrees of prominence required by the original.

A further factor now awaits attention. How quickly is the information to be presented? Wonderly (1968, p. 183) says that participants, events, and abstractions "may be thought of as constituting a quantity of information which 'flows' through the channel as the discourse proceeds." But at what speed should the information flow? Most translators can probably remember teachers or lecturers who packed so much information into an hour that the most diligent notetaker was hard pressed to keep up. On the other end of the scale are those teachers who seem to be able to talk more or less indefinitely, but convey only a small quantity of information in the process. These, then, are the two extremes: on the one hand, close-packed information, concentrated into the minimum of words, with little redundancy or repetition; on the other, information conveyed slowly, with a great deal of redundancy, and administered to the hearer in very diluted doses. Note that the actual information conveyed may be the same in both cases; it is not a question of *what* information is conveyed, but *at what speed* it is conveyed. We are not here dealing with content, but with rate.

At what speed, then, should the translator choose to convey his message? Nida and Taber (1969) say that a translation should "present the Biblical information at the rate at which they (the speakers of the RL) are accustomed to receive it." Different languages communicate information at different rates,[1] and the information rate in any given RL may differ considerably from that of Hebrew and Greek. This implies, of course, that the translator should be aware of the rate at which information may be acceptably communicated in the language into which he is translating.

Most of this chapter will be concerned with factors to which the translator should be alert, when trying to present the information of the original at a speed acceptable in the RL. A final section will be concerned, not with the rate at which information is presented, but with the information-value inherent in certain constructions. These two factors combine to form characteristic information patterns in each language, and a good translation will follow these patterns.

Known and new information

The organization of information into a discourse may be viewed in the following way. Certain items of information, often introducing the main topic or the chief participants, are mentioned first. In many languages, specific grammatical constructions are used at this point. This initial material forms a body of "known" information which is then assumed to be available to the listener or reader: from there the speaker goes on to present further information that is "new." The new information is not unrelated information, however; it is all connected in some way with the material already known. Once presented, this new information becomes a part of the reservoir of known information. The speaker now assumes that the hearer knows it, and he refers back to it, or in other ways assumes its content, in later parts of the discourse. Thus each bit of information added to a discourse contains some new element, but

---

[1] Nida and Taber (1969, p. 163) disagree here. They state, "From all the evidence we have it is also assumed that most languages have approximately the same rate of flow of information for corresponding types of style and levels of usage." The fact that a good translation tends very often to be longer than the original they attribute to the necessity of making explicit in the RL much that is implicit in the original. Until detailed studies of information structure become available, there may be inadequate evidence to settle this point, but it seems at least possible, and perhaps likely, that other factors as well as explicitness contribute to the greater length of the RL version. A language with a slow information rate (i.e., with more words per given quantity of information) may not necessarily be more explicit, but simply more repetitive, than the original.

is related in some way to what is already known; and once presented, that information is assumed to be "known."

In English we can signal what part of a sentence contains new information by the intonation we use. For instance, we can distinguish the following two sentences: "The student, who had failed his exams, remained remarkably cheerful," and "The student who had failed his exams remained remarkably cheerful." In the first sentence we give a separate intonation contour to the relative clause, and thereby imply that the information that the student had failed his exams was something new, previously unknown to the hearer. This sentence could equally well have been broken down into two shorter ones: "The student failed his exams. However, he remained remarkably cheerful." The second sentence, which does not separate off the relative clause intonationally, implies that the student's failing his exams was already known to the hearer, and is referred back to at this point simply to distinguish this particular student from others: The student who had failed his exams was cheerful, while some other students were not.

When referring to objects or participants, English signals them as either known or new by the use of the definite or indefinite article or the equivalent. Thus referring to "*a* woman" or "*some* women" implies that they are new to the discourse, whereas "*the* woman" or "*those* women" imply a previous mention — they are known.

Within the structure of the English clause, the new information is normally found in the predicate, and this is signaled as new by intonation, as stated above. For instance, a newlywed may say to a friend, "My mother-in-law's visit went off very well." The new information is the success of the visit, and the newlywed is obviously assuming her friend already knew that the visit had been made, or at least planned. The new information ("went off very well") forms the predicate, and the already-known information, the subject. However, if the newlywed knew her friend was quite unaware of the visit, she would present that also as new information, and say, "My mother-in-law visited us last week. It went off very well." If she wrongly thought that her friend knew of the proposed visit, and then realized her mistake, she might say something like this: "My mother-in-law's visit went off very well. Oh, did you not know she was coming? Yes, she came last week." In the first sentence the fact of the visit is assumed to be known: in the second the assumption is recognized as false and withdrawn:

in the third the information which had already been passed on, but in the form of known information, is now explicitly restated as new information. This shows that the distinction between known and new information is one to which English speakers react, and that different forms of presentation are recognized as appropriate to the two different kinds of information.

Detailed studies of information structure in languages other than English are still scarce, but it is safe to say that patterns of known and new information do exist in all languages, and that it is these patterns which an acceptable translation should reproduce. Obviously a language with a slow information rate will have a high proportion of known to new information. On the other hand, a rapid information rate will be characterized by a high quantity of new information compared to known. Whether the overall rate is slow or rapid, there will be characteristic ways of presenting information; each language has a selection of acceptable information patterns. Some of these will be studied in the remainder of the chapter, focusing attention first on known and then on new information.

Linking new to known information in discourse

It was stated earlier that in a well-formed discourse new information does not stand on its own, it is always connected in some way with the already known material which has preceded it. New material may be related back to the known by signals of various kinds. Reference back to a previously mentioned participant may be made by the use of pronouns, verb affixes, articles and demonstratives, ellipsis, or connectives. Whichever form is used in a particular language, the function is the same: it relates new information to someone already known in the narrative, saying in effect, "same participant as before." Events also may be referred back to, or mentioned twice: examples can be found in chapter 3.

Three devices will be described here which are commonly used to "plug in" new information to the appropriate part of the known, though it must not be thought that these three exhaust the field. The devices are connectives; affixation for gender, case, etc.; and repetition, whether exact or approximate.

Connectives. Crowell (1973, p. 17), describing information structure in Bororo (Brazil), says "Connectives keep the listener oriented as to sequential time, temporal setting, locational setting, logical connections, and nominal identity. This is done by relating new information to points that are already established in time, location, or nominal identity." Thus the basic time-space setting is normally given early in the discourse, and later change in time or space is signaled with reference to these, and signaled, in Bororo, by connectives. Probably the most common use of connectives is to establish logical relationships: Greek certainly uses connectives for both logical and chronological relationships. But other languages which make less use of connectives have to signal the same relationships, but in some other way. New information must still be clearly related to known, by whatever means.

Affixation for gender, case, etc. is also a common way of relating new to known material. In some languages, certainly, affixes may provide new information. But much more commonly affixes refer to something already known in the discourse. Thus nouns, adjectives, and demonstratives may carry affixes which signal both their relationship with each other, and their relationship with the verb. Verbs may carry affixes which indicate the relationship with preceding and following verbs, as well as with certain nouns in the sentence.

Greek was rich in such affixes, and hence was a language in which the relationship of new to known information was particularly clearly signaled. When read in a fairly literal translation, it often appears as if Greek had a rapid information rate: new information comes across in a concentrated and complex way. Pending adequate studies of Greek information patterns, it might be premature to comment on this. But certainly the complexities contained within a Greek sentence were considerably clarified for the original reader by the very full affixial system; every word, except for connectives and prepositions, carried endings which signaled exactly its relationship with what had preceded. These new-to-known linkages, however, are quite untranslatable in many languages, with the result that literal translations of the Greek tend to have too heavy a concentration of new information — heavier than Greek itself, and far too heavy for the language concerned. And the reason is simply that the new information could be transferred readily to another language, whereas much of the linking material could not. But in such cases, the RL will always have its own patterns for linking new material to known, and these should be followed. The content of the original must be transferred intact, and if this is to be done clearly then new material must be accompanied by an adequate amount of known, expressed appropriately.

Often translators find that to present the content of the original clearly they have to slow down the information rate, relative to the Greek, and deliberately build in more known information as they present the new. In many languages, an appropriate method of linking new material to known is by repetition, and this will now be considered.

Repetition. The term *repetition* is here used to mean much more than simply saying the same thing twice: it means referring to the same event twice, whether the same words are repeated or not.

There are many different ways of referring to the same event twice. First, of course, there is exact repetition. "They all *stopped talking* at once. When they had *stopped* . . . ." Alternatively, the second mention of the event may be by means of a pro-verb. "They all *stopped talking* at once. When they had *done so* . . . ."

Aguaruna of Peru uses both methods, but in different semantic circumstances. There is a very common pro-verb, *do thus,* but it is never used for events involving speaking or moving from place to place: for these, the verb is repeated. Thus we have ". . . he said. When *he said* . . . ." and "He went. Having *gone* . . . ." but ". . . he hit him. Having *done thus* . . . ." and ". . . he ate supper. Having *done thus* . . . ." Still other methods of referring to an event twice are available in many languages. The second mention, for example, may be replaced by a synonymous expression, one that uses different words to say exactly the same thing. "They all *stopped talking* at once. When they had *fallen silent* . . . ." Other possible restatement patterns are generic-specific, specific-generic, or positive-negated antonym. An example of the latter would be, "She fell silent at once; she didn't utter another word."

Whatever form of repetition is used, the effect is always the same. The second mention of the event provides virtually no new information in itself, hence it slows down the information rate considerably. Languages which use a great deal of repetition obviously have a spread-out rather than a compact information structure. But, quite apart from the form of repetition which is preferred in a particular language, there are also various purposes for which repetition is used, or, more accurately, there are various functions within discourse which repetition fulfills. These will now be discussed.

Some languages use repetition frequently for *amplification.* Here the second mention of the event is used as a vehicle for carrying some added information, some new material that was not mentioned the first time. Thus in Luke 8:23, the single Greek verb *suneplērounto* (translated in the TEV as "the boat began to fill with water") comes out in Walmatjari (Australia) as "The water was rising up. The water was filling up the boat." This presents the same information as the Greek verb, but more slowly: to give all the information only once would be too quick in Walmatjari.

As mentioned earlier, in several Australian languages information is often presented in a cyclic form. This may be seen in the following example, also from Walmatjari. Mark 12:41 reads, "And Jesus sat over against the treasury, and beheld how the people cast money into the treasury." The Walmatjari version reads, "When Jesus was sitting in God's house, men and women were going through. They were putting in money for God. As they were going they were putting it into a vessel for money. Jesus was sitting looking at them." This could be analyzed, information-wise, as A' B' B' ' B' ' ' A' ', thus:

A'   When Jesus was sitting in God's house

B'   Men and women were going through

B' '   They were putting in money for God

B' ' ' As they were going they were putting it into a vessel for money

A' '   Jesus was sitting looking at them.

In this analysis A' and A' ' both refer to Jesus, B', B' ', and B' ' ' all refer to the people who were putting money in. Note the steady build-up of information through B', B' ', and B' ' '. Note also the repetition of "Jesus was sitting" in A' ', forming the link with A' and completing the cyclic pattern.

Often repetition in some form is used as *a linking feature*. It does not then act as a vehicle for adding extra information, as above, but simply links the discourse together and, of course, slows up the communication rate in the process. Several examples from New Guinea languages were quoted in chapter 1. Ampale and Daga were quoted as using repetition to form linkage within the paragraph, while Kosena uses the same device to provide linkage between paragraphs. Examples could be multiplied from all over the world, though always with some distinctive characteristics also. In Shipibo (Peru) sentence-initial repetition using a participle is employed to signal continuity of participant as subject, change of subject being marked by certain connectives instead. Thus Matthew 19:3 reads, "The Pharisees came to Jesus. Having come they wanted to test him. Wanting to test him, one said, 'Is it lawful for a man to put away his wife . . . ?'" Note that in this language, the narrowing of focus from a group to one member of it (*"they* wanted to test him . . . *one* said . . .") counts as continuity of participant as subject. Shipibo cannot say *"they* said," like Greek does, when it is obvious that the Pharisees did not in fact speak in chorus, but that one of them was spokesman. But the united character of their approach to Jesus, signaled in Greek by the plural subject, is signaled in Shipibo by the participial repetition; there is no change of participant, only a change of focus.

Kasem (Ghana) uses a similar linking construction sentence-initial, but unlike Shipibo, cannot use it for events which follow each other in rapid succession. The use of a linking repetition in Kasem normally implies the end of one event-cluster and the beginning of the next.

Often, of course, the translator has the choice of whether or not to introduce such repetitions. In Waffa (New Guinea) narrative paragraphs could either be translated as one long sentence, without repetitions, or broken up into separate short sentences linked by repetitions. In such situations the reaction of language helpers and early readers often decides the issue. In this case the translators tended to use the more broken-up, repetitive style when the paragraph presented much unfamiliar material, proper names, or included clauses. Thus Mark 7:31-33 in Waffa reads, "Jesus returned and came again from the town called Tyre, passed through the town called Sidon, passed through the big town called Decapolis and came and sat on the bank of lake Galilee. He sat, and the friends of a man who was deaf and could not talk got him and went to Jesus. They went, and strongly asked Jesus to touch him. When they had asked him, Jesus . . . ." All this could equally well have been presented as one long sentence, but the information load would then have been heavier.

Longacre (1968) points out the important part played by repetition in paragraph linkage. The first sentence of a paragraph may repeat, more or less exactly, either the first or the last sentence of the preceding paragraph; alternatively, it may summarize the content of that paragraph as a whole. Sometimes a paragraph-initial sentence refers back to the theme of the total discourse.

Kayapo (Brazil) provides an interesting example of large-scale repetition. At the end of an episode a transition paragraph occurs consisting entirely of repetitive material, acting as an introduction to the next episode. Stout and Thomson (1971, p. 254) state, *"Tran-*

sition paragraphs are repetitions of two or more sentences, either verbatim or in general meaning, from the previous base paragraph . . . . New vocabulary is occasionally introduced in the transition paragraph to add color to the description; but it may not add information consisting of actual events, as does the base paragraph."

The above examples serve to underline the fact that while many languages use repetition for linkage, different verbs or clauses will be repeated in different languages, with differing significance. Care must be taken to use repetition at the right points.

However, it must not be thought that all repetition involves events. Hebrew, for instance, was highly repetitive in its use of personal and locative names. Mention has already been made of its frequent use of personal names (chapter 3). An example of repetition of locational reference is found in Genesis 21:31-33a: "Therefore that place was called Beersheba, because there both of them swore an oath. So they made a covenant at Beersheba. Then Abimelech and Phicol the commander of his army rose up and returned to the land of the Philistines. Abraham planted a tamarisk tree in Beersheeba . . . ." Many languages could not naturally repeat the same place name three times in one paragraph: a device that signaled cohesion and slowed down the information rate in Hebrew would simply cause confusion in another language, where the information rate would be, in that respect, faster. Mention of a location paragraph-initial would establish that location as unchanged until a specific change was stated.

Another kind of repetition which differs from both the amplifying and linking types is the repetition involved in *preview and summary*. These are like opposite sides of a coin: in a preview you announce what you are going to say before you say it, while in a summary you briefly recapitulate afterwards what you have already said.

Cromack (1968, p. 277) describing Cashinawa discourse structure, describes the function of preview thus. "The linguistic device used to avoid creating suspense is the use of *preview* and *pick-up*. Preview is the linguistic expression of events which are going to be realized on the predication-line in the text, but before the temporally appropriate position. Pick-up is the final predication of the previewed event. (Cf. predication and flashback.) The purpose of preview is generally to identify participants with regard to their involvement in the story and thus to avoid suspense." Thus in Cashinawa discourse an event may be mentioned ahead of time, i.e., before it is actually asserted on the time-line. Cromack goes on to give examples showing that the use of preview varies according to the discourse type concerned: explanatory discourse uses frequent preview and consequently has no element of suspense, while folk tales use no long-term preview at all, and suspense is kept high to the end of the story.

Preview in narrative discourse is often contained in included speech or purpose clauses: an intention is first stated and then carried out, as in John 19:38-40. It is also used, as described above for Cashinawa, to give a significant identification: see Matthew 10:4 ("Judas Iscariot who also betrayed him").

Examples so far have been concerned with preview of a time-line event, but in fact, as Cromack indicated for Cashinawa, it is more common, and occurs with wider functions, in explanatory and hortatory material. A preview of a theme-line event is normally given for one of two reasons: (1) to keep the theme clearly in view when there is much detail or background material. (2) when the grammar of the RL necessitates the presentation of a main clause before dependent material, or in some way differs markedly from the grammar of the original.

Summary is a type of brief, generalized repetition. It is used in many languages to distinguish thematic from background material. But a summary frequently signals closure also, often the end of a paragraph, while in other languages it simply serves to focus attention on what is crucial to the argument.

Greek discourse structure was able to carry a great deal of detail and illustrative material along with the main theme, often even in the same clause. But in many cases the RL cannot do this; in fact there are few languages which can carry the amount of information in one clause that Greek could. Thus translators often have to make use of preview and/or summary to keep the theme-line clear and the grammar within the bounds of naturalness.

An example using both preview and summary is the Huixteco version of Romans 8:38, 39. (". . . neither death, nor life, nor angels, nor principalities . . . shall be able to separate us from the love of God, which is in Christ Jesus our Lord.") Huixteco cannot launch into such a list without first saying what the list is about, so v. 38 therefore starts, "not even a little can anything separate us and God." There follows the list, which is concluded by a final summary, "God is with us forever, He who loves us on account of our Lord Jesus Christ."

Similar methods may be used with different kinds of theme to make them easier to follow. For example, 1 Peter 3:3, 4 contains a long contrast with considerable detail given on each side: "³Whose adorning let it not be that outward adorning of plaiting the hair, and of wearing of gold, or of putting on of apparel; ⁴But let it be the hidden man of the heart, in that which is not corruptible, even the ornament of a meek and quiet spirit, which is in the sight of God of great price." In Tzutujil (Guatemala) it was found advisable to use a preview in translating these verses, otherwise the reader might have read all of v. 3 before realizing that a contrast was being made at all. It is much more natural in that language to state the contrast succinctly in one short sentence, and then add the detail later, thus, "Don't set your heart on dressing yourselves up more than on having a good inner life. Don't set your heart a lot on fixing up your hair or on things made of gold or on expensive clothes. But what is necessary is a good inner life . . . ." The preview sentence here derives one-half of the contrast from v. 3 and the other from v. 4. Then the specific detail of each half is handled in turn, the preview providing the known background against which the specific new information can be understood. It is important to note that preview and summary convey no extra information over and above what is conveyed by the original; they simply convey existing information *more than once*, to facilitate understanding and increase naturalness in a language with a slower information rate.

Yet another way in which repetition is used to spread the communication load is when *listing* is involved. Listing occurs when a number of things (or propositions) stand in the same relationship to a given event: some languages only need to state the event and relationship once, and then list all the things, while other languages have to repeat the event with each thing. Hebrew and Greek both use a listing construction quite readily, but in translation this often has to be spread out. Thus in Cashinawa (Peru) Genesis 1:12 reads, "The earth instrumentally caused vegetation to rise, caused vegetables with seed to rise, caused trees with fruit to rise, their fruit having seed; this done, God looked and it was good."

Greek not only uses lists readily, but packs a great deal of information into them by the use of abstract nouns and participles. The "unpacking" of this information so that it may be presented naturally in the RL often requires that the meaning of abstract nouns be spelled out in full, and the relationship with the shared event

stated each time as well. An example of this is found in the Huixteco version of Romans 8:38, 39, the preview and summary of which
were quoted in an earlier paragraph. Huixteco cannot simply list
"neither death, nor life, nor angels, nor principalities, etc." without
making the full relationship explicit each time, thus, "Whether we
die or whether we live, we and God will not separate. Even if
those who have power like an angel or a devil want to separate us
and God, we can't be separated. If there is something that takes
place now or on another day, we will not separate." Note that
unlike the Cashinawa, which repeated "to cause to rise" with each
item in the list, Huixteco style prefers a more varied wording, rather
than exact repetition. Thus we have, "We and God will not separate . . . we can't be separated . . . we will not separate . . . ."

Repetition is also used in translation *to keep the theme-line clear*
where either the compactness or the abundance of information in
the Greek would tend to obscure the thrust of the message. An
example is 1 Peter 1:18, 19, which form part of a longer Greek
sentence. These verses read, "Ye know that ye were not redeemed
with corruptible things, as silver and gold, from your vain conversation received by tradition from your fathers; but with the precious
blood of Christ, as of a lamb without blemish and without spot."
The *theme* of these two verses may be stated quite simply, "You
were redeemed, not with corruptible things, but with the blood of
Christ." All the other information is illustrative, and describes
some element contained in the theme, telling either how, or from
what, the believers were delivered. Obviously, then, the central
event in these verses is "redeemed," to which all the rest of the
information relates, either directly or indirectly. But in many languages it is not possible to present this quantity of information all
attaching to the one item; the reader loses the thread, and by the
time he gets to the end he has no idea to what preceding "known"
he should attach the later information. There may not even exist in
the language any way of signaling the relationship of a clause to
some other item quite far removed from it in the discourse. The
solution, then, is to keep on referring back to the "known" item at
intervals, either by repeating it exactly, or by using synonyms, or
by using cross-referent terms such as pronouns, demonstratives, or
pro-verbs. Using these verses as an example, an approach using
demonstratives and pro-verbs would have the structure, "*You were
redeemed* from your futile way of life . . . . *This* was not *accomplished* by the payment of silver and gold. God *did it* by the

payment of the precious blood of Christ." Kekchi (Guatemala) prefers exact repetition: "You know that *you are redeemed* from the worthless way that you were taught by your ancestors. *You are not redeemed* with that which ends like silver and gold. But *you are redeemed* by means of the precious blood of the Lord Jesus Christ." English prefers to use synonyms or synonymous phrases, as in the NEB version, "Well you know that it was no perishable stuff, like gold or silver, that *bought your freedom* from the empty folly of your traditional ways. *The price was paid* in precious blood . . . ." English is in fact a language which allows any of the above three ways of referring back to the "known," and in addition has the other option in the Greek, that of referring to the "known" only once and making all related information dependent on that one reference. But most languages are more restricted than English in this: given a great deal of information relating back to one "known," only one or two of the four possibilities mentioned would be available and desirable. The translator must be sensitive to how much information may be hung from one peg, as it were; and when the limit is reached, he must know the most natural means of reintroducing the "known" into the discourse.

Patterns of new information in discourse

If it is true that known information occurs in discourse in certain recognizable patterns, this is equally true of new information. Unfortunately this subject has received little attention as yet, so only a few guidelines may here be given. It is hoped they will be sufficient to stimulate further study.

Cromack (1968, p. 40, footnote) says, "There are frequency restrictions controlling the amount of . . . information which is generally included in a given . . . phrase or . . . clause. And there are specific mechanisms whereby additional information may be included in the text without expanding any construction beyond its expected dimensions. Much research remains to be done in this area."

Several questions will be posed here, which each investigator will have to answer for his own language. Is there any obvious pattern of known and new information in relation to the larger grammatical units, discourse and paragraph? What parts of the sentence may carry a heavy load of new information? What parts of the clause typically carry known information, and what parts new? If additional information has to be incorporated beyond what a construction may carry, how is this done? Brief comments will be made on each of these questions in turn.

Is there any obvious pattern of known and new information in relation to discourse and paragraph? As has already been mentioned, there is usually a heavy concentration of new information early in the discourse. Different languages employ different devices at this point. Bororo (Brazil) uses short sentences in the introduction to a discourse, in which information is repeated several times. Kasem (Ghana), also uses short sentences in discourse introductions, but does not repeat information more than once. There is a strong tendency in Kasem introductory sentences for the information to be carried in the nominal rather than the verbal elements of the sentence, while the reverse is true in the main flow of the discourse.

Within the paragraph, it has been noted for Karan (New Guinea) that the topic sentence, at or near the beginning of the paragraph, carried more information than sentences in the body of the paragraph. Since this does not seem to have been the pattern in the New Testament Greek, the danger obviously arises of trying to pack too much information into paragraph-medial sentences.

What parts of the sentence may carry a heavy load of new information? It seems almost certain that the main clause of a sentence may always carry new information: the question remains as to how much can be carried in the various types of subordinate clause. Hebrew and Greek both seem to have been able to carry a great deal of new information in subordinate clauses. Exodus 1:10 contains the reported speech, "Let us deal shrewdly with them, lest they multiply, and lest, if war befall, they join our enemies." Many languages would be quite unable to present so much new information in subordinate clauses. Ways would have to be found of presenting the same items of information, with the same relationships between them, but using more main and less subordinate clauses. Details would vary with the language, but something along the following lines might meet the conditions: "I fear lest this people may multiply. If war comes, perhaps they will join our enemies. Therefore let us deal shrewdly with them."

Greek also could carry a great deal of information in subordinate clauses. John 21:20 contains an identifying flashback in the form of a long relative clause, which reads, "Who also leaned on his breast at supper and said, 'Lord, who is he who betrays you?'" This identifies a particular disciple by referring back to a previous occasion and describing both his position and what he said at that time. But Bahnar (Vietnam) cannot include so much information in a relative clause. It therefore rewords the information as follows: "The one who sat near Jesus and asked Jesus a while back. He said, 'Lord, who will betray you?' He asked that when they ate together a while back." All the same information is included here, but it is more broken up, and presented in main clauses. The final repetitive sentence, "He asked that when they ate together a while back" serves a double purpose: first, it carries the new information "when they ate together" (Greek *en tō deipnō*) embedded in known information, rather than adding to the load of a previous sentence, and second, it binds the whole flashback into a unity, and signals its closure, preparatory to returning to the time-line of the narrative in the next sentence.

What parts of the clause typically carry known information, and what new? English, as has already been mentioned, normally encodes new information into the predicate of the clause: the same is true in Kasem, where the subject place tends to be kept for known information, new information normally being conveyed in the verb with or without its object. The object place carries much more new information than either subject or indirect object: it is possible, for instance, to have a long list of participants in object position, whereas this virtually never occurs as subject of the clause. Indirect object place is normally filled only by a pronoun, very occasionally by a single noun, i.e., it normally carries only known information, and never much information of any kind. With this, contrast Exodus 1:15, "Then the king of Egypt said to the Hebrew midwives, one of whom was named Shiphrah and the other Puah." Obviously it is not possible to transfer all this information into indirect object place in Kasem. The new information must be put into the appropriate (here non-verbal or stative) clause types, thus, "There were two midwives of the Hebrews. One was called Shiphrah. The other was called Puah. At that time the king of Egypt said to them . . . ." Translated in this way, the indirect object place contains only known information, in the form of a pronoun, following normal Kasem information patterns.

Munduruků (Brazil) distinguishes new and known participants by mentioning them in different positions in the clause. If the subject of the verb refers to a participant being introduced for the first time, it precedes the predicate; if the subject refers to a known participant, it occurs following the predicate (Sheffler, 1970, p. 31).

If additional information has to be incorporated beyond what a construction may carry, how is this done? This question cannot be answered unless another can be answered first — what kind of information? This question is dealt with more fully later in this chapter. It is sufficient to state here that different kinds of surplus information are incorporated into the discourse in different ways, in the same language: the translator has not one, but several devices at his disposal, of which he must choose whichever is appropriate.

Having said this, however, it must be made clear that many of the devices for distributing information into several units do have features in common, and some of these will now be considered.

If a Greek or Hebrew construction carries an information load too heavy for the RL, some alternative solutions are (1) to split it up into smaller units using repetition as a linkage, (2) to split it up using implied information (including implied relationships) as a linkage, (3) to split it into several shorter constructions, in such a way that no additional linkage is needed, (4) to split it up into more units using semantically neutral or "dummy" words to carry the extra information.

(1) *Splitting an original construction into smaller units using repetition as linkage.* A clause in Romans 6:23 reads, "For the wages of sin is death." The occurrence of abstract nouns here means that much information is communicated in a few words; the Huixteco therefore redistributes the same information as follows, "Because the one who works for sin, he will be paid for his work. The payment of his work will be that he will be lost eternally." Here the first sentence covers "wages of sin," and the second, "is death." The nominalized repetition of "paid for his work" links the two together.

(2) *Splitting an original construction into smaller units in such a way that no additional linkage is needed.* It is often true that simply to divide out information into smaller chunks somehow makes it easier to absorb. Thus Matthew 8:4 ("See thou tell no man; but go thy way, shew thyself to the priest, and offer the gift that Moses commanded, for a testimony unto them"), is translated into Shipibo by three separate sentences, without any extra linking material being needed. "See that you tell no one. Go your way to show yourself to the priest. So that they may know that you are healed, offer the gift that Moses commanded."

(3) *Splitting an original construction into smaller units using*

implied information as linkage. In Kasem, Luke 15:12 ("Father, give me the portion of goods that falleth to me," (one clause in Greek)), becomes "Father, take your possessions and divide, result you give me my share." Here "dividing" as an event is implied in "portion of goods," and of course the giving of the share is dependent on the dividing taking place first, hence the use of "result."

(4) *Splitting an original construction into more units using semantically neutral words.* The Kasem example just quoted also illustrates this further device for load-spreading. The verb "take" in Kasem occurs commonly in combination with some other verb, and has almost no information value on its own. It is virtually a dummy verb, with the sole function of carrying the object and certain grammatical signals. The verb which does carry information, i.e., "divide," is hence unburdened by either. In most northern Ghanaian languages it is too much to introduce a participant, location or time, and a significant event, in one clause. In the Gur group of languages a common pattern is, "A certain man *rose up* one day, and went hunting." Bisa, of a different language family, would say *sat down.* In neither case is there any reference to his actual movements, the verbs are dummy verbs to carry the participant and temporal information. Thus in Luke 10:31 ("And by chance there came down a certain priest that way") is translated in Kasem, "*There was* a certain priest, he *got up* and came down that road." The verbs *there was* and *got up* carry no meaning of their own, they are used to spread the information load. Note that the words "by chance" have been intentionally omitted: to include them in Kasem would have given the impression the priest himself had not intended to go that way, i.e., they would have conveyed wrong information.

The above offers some hope that quantity-of-new-information may prove to be a contributory factor in sentence length. But documented studies in this field are urgently needed.

Patterns of expected information in discourse

To call all information either "known" or "new," as has been done so far in this chapter, is a useful oversimplification. There are times when the distinction is rather hard to apply. This happens when the context arouses a strong expectation of certain information, as "fish and . . ." invites the addition of "chips," or "Be quiet, Mummy's got a . . ." implies "headache," at least to a noisy child. When such strongly anticipated information is in fact presented, it scarcely counts as "new." Since it was expected anyway, it adds almost nothing to the information load.

Expected information does not cause any difficulty to the translator, or the reader, as long as it occurs according to expectation. The problem arises when information which is strongly expected in the RL is not stated in the original. If the reader expects information which is not given, he suddenly finds himself pulled up short; the information load is too heavy, or too confused, and he has to ask questions to sort out the situation.

The examples above may have given the impression that certain collocations of words give rise to the expectation of some other specific word, that it is simply a lexical matter. But such examples show only half the picture: it is not only certain words, but certain categories of information, that can be strongly expected, and expected almost to the point of being obligatory. Let us assume two people conversing. The speaker may have a language background which says, "Given information X and Z, Y can of course be assumed." The hearer may come from a background which says that if X, Y and Z occurred all must be stated. So if the speaker says "X, Z," (meaning of course "X, Y, Z,") the hearer may well react by saying "not Y? But why not?" Put briefly, what can be implied in one language may have to be stated in another, and vice versa.

The whole area of expected information awaits serious research. Problems for the translator seem to lie mostly in those situations where Greek could imply information which requires explicit statement in the RL. If the translator is also able to omit the same information in his own mother tongue, he is especially liable to translate the Greek as it stands without realizing that the RL needs to have the implied information overtly presented.

Take, for example, Mark 2:1. "And again he entered Capernaum after some days; and it was noised that he was in the house." This is clear enough, in Greek and in English — but in some languages it would provoke the response, "What house?" In such languages, change of location must be stated explicitly. If you say he entered Capernaum, you mean he entered the town; if you mean that he then entered a house, you must say so. In Huixteco, it is not possible to mention the house at all without saying *whose* house, in this case the very indefinite *"someone's house."*

In both Greek and Hebrew it was possible to omit a verb of motion, if it was clear from the context that motion actually took place. In many West African languages, on the other hand, any motion that took place must be stated. In the story of Moses in the bulrushes, Exodus 2:3 reads, "she took for him an ark . . . and put the child therein; and she laid it in the flags by the river's brink." Motion is implied in the last clause of the verse; Moses' mother had to go to the river to leave the child there. This is clear, were proof needed, from vv. 7 and 8. Moses' sister said, "Shall I *go* and call thee a nurse . . . ?" She then *went* and called the child's mother. Thus it is obvious that their home was not right at the water's edge — motion was involved. In Kasem, motion is not normally implied, but stated, so the last clause of the verse becomes, "she *went* to the river's brink and laid it in the flags." This is not only more natural, and avoids confusion; it also spreads out the information in a more acceptable way. To attach both "in the flags" and "by the river's brink" to the single verb "laid" would be too heavy an information load in Kasem.

Other examples of information which cannot be omitted may also be illustrated from Ghanaian languages. In Luke 17:7 Jesus points out that a man does not wait on his servant at the end of the day's work, but expects the servant to wait on him. The master does not say to the servant, "Come at once and sit down at table." Obviously, the hypothetical invitation is to eat, not simply to sit down — but in Kasem an implied purpose must be stated, and therefore the invitation has to state explicitly, "Come at once and sit at table *that you may eat.*" In Tampulma, another language of Ghana, an implied purpose similarly has to be made explicit, and Matthew 20:32 ("And Jesus stood still and called them") becomes, "Jesus stood and called them *that they come.*"

Another kind of information which may never be left implied in Kasem is instrument. Thus Mark 14:47, ("One of those who stood by drew his sword, and struck the slave of the high priest,") has to be expanded thus, ". . . drew his sword *and used it* and struck the slave . . . ."

Many of these "obligatory additions" seem trivial to English speakers, who would readily assume them anyway. But in a language where these items are strongly expected, their omission causes confusion, and hence adds to the information load.

Turning to another part of the world, different examples are found of the same kind of problem. In Shipibo (Peru), if a command is reported in a discourse, the response to that command must also be reported, in equal detail. Thus Matthew 9:6 reads,

"Jesus said to him, Having arisen and taking up your bed, go home. And so he arose. Having arisen he took up his bed. Taking up his bed he went home." On occasions, omitting to report the response to a command may lead not only to information overload, but to wrong interpretation. Matthew 22:4, 5 reads, "Again he sent other servants, saying, 'Tell those who are invited, Behold I have made ready my dinner, etc., and everything is ready; come to the marriage feast.' But they made light of it and went off . . . ." The Shipibos are so accustomed to expect a command to be followed by the response to it, that they interpret these verses after the same pattern, assuming it was not the guests but the servants who made light of the intending host's instructions and went off.

In the same language it is impossible to handle logical argument in the way Greek does. In Greek it is possible to state the premises of an argument, and leave the conclusion to be inferred, but in Shipibo the conclusion also must be stated explicitly. Thus in the story of the temptation, Matthew 4:4 has to be expanded to include the conclusion of the argument as well. "Then he said, 'It is written, Men shall live not by bread alone. They shall live by every word that proceeds from God's mouth. Therefore I will not command the stones to become bread,' unquote he said."

There is no suggestion in this chapter that information *not* implied in the original should be included in the RL simply for the sake of naturalness. But if information is implied in the original, the translator must ask himself several questions. (1) If I omit this information, would my readers assume it to be implied? (2) If they would not, then would they find the omission jarring or confusing? (3) If this information is omitted, does it make the information load too heavy at some other point?

INFORMATION VALUE

Every grammatical construction is used not only to convey information, but to carry a certain kind of information. It is not enough for the translator to be able to distinguish a well-formed construction from an "ungrammatical" one; he must also know what kind of information a given construction conveys. And this requires conscious investigation and control, outside the domain of syntax, but related to syntactic constructions and signals of different kinds.

An illustration may help here. In Kasem the predominant construction in narrative is the clause series, that is, a main clause followed by a series of secondary clauses, all having considerable restrictions as to tense, etc.; the same participant is the grammatical subject of all clauses in the series. Given a detailed description of the restrictions, the translator may obviously weed out from his translation any series which breaks the rules. But this is not usually the problem. The problem is, when do I use such a series and when do I not? In fact this construction is used only for chronologically-ordered events performed by the same participant, *which together form a larger grouping*; that is, the events are related by something more than just the agent and the time-line, they form a single event cluster. A marked time-lapse or a change of objective both serve to terminate the series and start a new series, even though chronological ordering and agent remain constant.

A similar example may be quoted from Shipibo (Peru), where two constructions are possible when the same agent performs successive events. The first construction, ("Agent did; having done X he did Y"), implies events in one event cluster, without any long time-lapse. The other construction, ("Agent did X. Then that man did Y"), is used when the second event marks the start of a new activity-span.

Thus it can be seen that certain grammatical constructions are appropriate in certain semantic contexts, and by virtue of this fact carry semantic overtones over and above the participants and related events which form their content. Several examples of constructions which are used in specific semantic circumstances may be found in other chapters. Some constructions typically carry known rather than new information, others imply either assertion or hypothesis, change of participant as agent, change of focus, etc. Constructions should be used in translation, therefore, only in the appropriate semantic circumstances.

A detailed example will be provided here, to illustrate a type of analysis that may be applied to any construction.

An analysis of the information-value of "when" clauses in Kasem yielded these results:

1. *When* clauses most commonly carry no new information at all; they are an exact or near exact repetition of the preceding clause, and act as a linking device introducing a new activity-span, often a new paragraph.
2. *When* clauses carrying no new information, but with variations in wording, occur after a fairly long stretch of background material, to indicate that the narrative is now returning to the time-line.

3. *When* clauses may carry new *temporal* or *locational* information, provided the participant is known and the event known or expected.

4. *When* clauses may carry a heavy load of new information when the preceding part of the discourse describes a situation or activity that has continued for some time; then some cognition occurs which is the immediate cause of a change to a different activity or situation. In these semantic circumstances, the cognition clause is cast as a *when* clause.

Given this information, let us turn to several verses in the New Testament using the Greek *hote*, "when," and see whether or not they may be translated by *when* in Kasem.

Matt. 13:26 "When the blade was sprung up, and brought forth fruit . . . ." Heavy load of new information: cannot be translated by Kasem *when*.

Acts 8:12 "When they believed Philip preaching the things concerning the kingdom of God, and the name of Jesus Christ . . . ." This does not contain new information — the fact that they had believed Philip's message is conveyed in v. 6, although the wording is slightly different. The intervening material in vv. 6b-8 is not on the time-line, containing explanatory material and summary, while vv. 9-11 form a flashback. Thus the *hote* clause at the beginning of v. 12 could appropriately be translated by a Kasem *when* clause, signaling return to the time-line.

Acts 11:2 "And when Peter was come up to Jerusalem . . . ." This contains new locational information, as in 3 above. But it also contains a new participant (i.e., not mentioned in the preceding sentence,) and the event was not known or expected, so *when* should not be used here.

Acts 21:5 "And when we had accomplished those days . . . ." New temporal information, no new participant or unexpected event. Therefore it can be translated by *when*.

Gal. 2:14 "But when I saw that they walked not uprightly according to the truth of the gospel . . . ." A cognition that led to a change in the situation; therefore, according to 4 above this may be translated by *when* in spite of the heavy information load.

With this example before us, several points deserve special comment.

1. A given construction in the original cannot always be translated by the same construction in the RL.

2. A wide variety of factors enter into the information-value of a grammatical construction — in the above example, time, place, and cognition were all relevant factors.

3. As was mentioned earlier, the various categories of discourse-value overlap. This one construction contributes to the discourse, (1) grouping — it initiates a new activity-span; (2) cohesion — it normally signals continuity of participant; and can also signal return to the time-line, i.e., event cohesion. (3) quantity of information — it normally conveys very little new information (4) value of information — it can convey certain types of information but not others.

4. It is noticeable that the most common use of Kasem *when*, the repetitive use with linking significance, does not appear at all in the above set of New Testament examples. Yet obviously, a discourse would not sound natural if the construction was used correctly where time, space, and cognition were involved, but never for linking purposes. The solution is, of course, to use *when* as a link whenever it is natural in the RL, that is, at the start of a new activity-span not involving change of participant. Notice that this is *not* putting in something that is not there in the Greek: it is simply putting in something that is not signaled by *when* in the Greek. Greek has its own way of signaling "same participant," (verb endings, participles, relative pronouns) and its own ways of starting a new activity-span (these may prove to be different with different Biblical writers). Where the Greek signals, in its own way, the information "same participant, new activity-span," then the Kasem translation should use the construction which has the same significance.

The Kasem example above provided an example of the semantic analysis of a *when* clause. *If* clauses in various languages also cause translation problems where they signal different discourse values from the Greek *ei* and *ean*, and related particles normally translated by "if." The most common problem is that in some languages an *if* construction is always hypothetical, i.e., the stated content may be true or it may not, and this uncertainty is inherent in the use of the construction itself. In Greek, however, the particle *ei* could be used when no doubt was being expressed at all, as in "If ye be risen with Christ, seek . . ." (Col. 3:1). In such cases, the best translation in many languages would be some construction meaning "In view of the fact that . . . ," or else a statement followed by "therefore": "You are risen with Christ, therefore seek . . . ."

The converse holds with unfulfilled conditions, such as is found in John 8:42, "Jesus said to them, 'If God were your Father, you would love me.'" This is just the opposite of the situation quoted above, in which the *if* clause contained information which was known to be true; in the case now quoted, the *if* clause contains information known to be false, the meaning being, "God is not your Father; and this is proved by the fact that you do not love me." This creates a problem in languages where *if* implies genuine doubt. In some cases the *if* construction has to be avoided; Nung (Vietnam) uses it, but has to preface it by "Oh, no . . . ," thus explicitly denying the Jewish claim that God was their Father.

In Greek, *if* clauses could be used equally well for a specific situation, ("If you had been here my brother would not have died," John 11:21), or for a generalized situation, ("I am the door; if anyone enters by me he will be saved," John 10:9). Gahuku (New Guinea) has no difficulty in translating the specific construction by "if," but translates the general one, "One who not bypassing me will enter . . . ."

Sometimes several implied meanings are involved in one verse, as in John 15:20, "If they persecuted me, they will perescute you; if they kept my word, they will keep yours also." Here the first *if* clause refers to a general situation rather than a specific event, and it implies information known to be true — Jesus had been persecuted. The second *if* clause is also general, but implies information known to be false — the Jews had not believed Christ's word. In neither case is there any uncertainty as to the truth of the statement; the relationship is one of comparison and consequence. Thus the Guhuku translation reads, "Since they continually put persecution to me, in just the same way they will surely put persecution to you too. Since they did not hear and put inside my talk, similarly they will surely not hear and put inside your talk."

Sometimes *if* introduces a purely hypothetical situation, introductory to stating its consequences. This does not imply any uncertainty, rather it says, "Let us assume that this hypothetical circumstance holds; in that case . . . ." An example of this is found in Luke 11:11, 12, "What father among you, *if* (1) his son asks for a fish, will instead of a fish give him a serpent; or *if* (2) he asks for an egg, will give him a scorpion? *If* (3) ye then being evil . . . ." Here *if* (1) and *if* (2) both mean "let us suppose that," while *if* (3) means "since," followed by a fact known to be true.

The truth or otherwise of a statement may be implied in other constructions, not only *if* clauses. This is particularly so with quotations and illustrations, but is also found with conjunctions. In an Aztec dialect of Mexico a conjunction meaning "but" carries the implied information that the preceding statement is untrue, and the following statement true. Thus it would be impossible to use this conjunction in such a verse as Romans 7:15, "For what I would, that do I not; *but* what I hate, that do I."

In Nung (Vietnam) quoted statements are understood to be true unless they are expressly marked as being untrue. No such mark, of course, is normally given in the original, so extra information has to be inserted to make sure that the quotation is not taken as a statement of fact. Thus the translation of Mark 3:22, "And the scribes . . . *spoke lying* and said, 'He hath Beelzebub.'" See also Mark 14:30, ". . . this night, before the cock crow twice, you shall *lie* three times saying you do not know me." The assessment of the truth or otherwise of the statement is made, not objectively, but from the point of view of whoever is speaking. Thus in John 19:7 (". . . he ought to die because he has made himself the Son of God,") the words "but he is not," had to be added to give the real meaning of the Jews. Obviously, if Jesus was truly the Son of God, as the unexpanded quotation would imply, then this was a singularly poor reason for saying that he ought to die. Equally obviously, the Jews thought they had strong grounds on their side: he ought to die because he falsely claimed to be God's Son. For the argument to make any sense, the implied assertion that his claim was false has to be made explicit.

In some languages illustrations have to be marked as such, or else they are taken as statements of fact. When the scribes and Pharisees criticized Christ for eating and drinking with sinners, (Mark 2:16, 17), he replied with an illustration, "They that are whole have no need of the physician, but they that are sick." Readers in White Tai (Vietnam) rightly equated Jesus with the physician, but understood him to be speaking literally, with the implication, "These people don't need me but the sick people do; where are the sick people for me to heal?" The problem was solved by signaling the illustration as such at the start; "I *give you an example*; people who are well . . . ."

It is equally possible to mark the discourse-value of the illustration in the introductory clause instead. This was done in the Halang (Vietnam) version of Mark 2:19: *"Jesus gave them an illustration,* 'Can the wedding guests fast . . . ?' "

CONCLUSION

When trying to make a translation in which all information is given the right discourse-value, and is expressed by the appropriate constructions, the translator is hampered by not having all the information available that he really needs. The discourse structure of Greek has not yet received adequate attention. In due course it is hoped that this lack will be supplied by propositional outlines, and by studies in the discourse-value of common Greek constructions.[2] Neither of these will be much help to the translator, however, if he is unaware of the discourse values of constructions in the RL. Thus at the present time a primary objective should be the study of RL grammars from the point of view of the meanings they express, and this may be done by analyzing each construction in terms of quantity and kind of information, as has been done in this chapter.

[2] Greenlee, in his Heidemann Lecture (1969) has some valuable comments on word order and emphasis in NT Greek, but nevertheless considers this an area which still needs the attention of descriptive linguists (*ibid.*, p. 6). More such studies in aspects of Greek discourse would be of great value to translators.

BIBLIOGRAPHY

The works cited in this bibliography are those which pertain directly to discourse studies. It presupposes the more general bibliography on translation theory found in *Translating the Word of God*.

Abrams, Norman. 1961. "Word Base Classes in Bilaan." *Lingua* 10:391-402.

Callow, Kathleen. 1970. "More on Propositions and their Relations within a Discourse." NOT 37:23-27.

Cromack, R. E. 1968. "Language Systems and Discourse Structure in Cashinawa." Ph.D. dissertation, Hartford Seminary Foundation.

Crowell, Thomas H. 1973. "Cohesion in Bororo Discourse." *Linguistics* 104: 15-27.

Duff, Martha. 1973. "Contrastive Features of Written and Oral Texts in Amuesha." NOT 50:2-13.

Edgerton, Faye. 1964. "Relative Frequency of Direct and Indirect Discourse." NOT 10: 7, 8.

Elkins, Richard E. 1970. "Major Grammatical Patterns of Western Bukidnon Manobo." *Summer Institute of Linguistics Publications in Linguistics and Related Fields, Publication Number 26.* Norman, Okla.: Summer Institute of Linguistics of the University of Oklahoma.

Greenlee, J. Harold. 1969. "The importance of syntax for the proper understanding of the sacred text of the New Testament." Heidemann Lectures. Concordia Theological Seminary. Springfield, Ill.

Grimes, Joseph E. 1972a. *The Thread of Discourse.* Technical report No. 1, National Science Foundation Grant GS-3180. Ithaca: Cornell University.

------. 1972b. "Outlines and Overlays." *Language* 48:513-24.

Grimes, Joseph E., and Glock, Naomi. 1970. "A Saramacan Narrative Pattern." *Language* 46:408-25.

Halliday, M. A. K. 1969. "Linguistic Function and Literary Style: an inquiry into the language of William Golding's *The Inheritors.*" To appear in the proceedings of the Second Style in Language Conference (Bellagio, 1969), ed., Seymour Chatman and published by the Oxford University Press, New York.

------. 1967-1968. "Notes on Transitivity and Theme in English." Parts 1, 2, and 3. *Journal of Linguistics 6* 3:37-81; 3:199-224; 4:179-216.

------. 1970a. "Functional Diversity in Language as seen from a Consideration of Modality and Mood in English." *Foundations of Language* 6:22-61.

————. 1970b. "The Place of 'Functional Sentence Perspective' in the System of Linguistic Description." Report prepared for International Symposium on Functional Sentence Perspective, Mariáuske Lázné, 12-14 October 1970.

Kingston, Peter K. E. 1973. "Repetition as a Feature of Discourse Structure in Mamaindé." NOT 50:13:22.

Larson, Mildred L. 1965. "A Method for Checking Discourse Structure in Bible Translation." NOT 17:1-25.

Lauriault, James. 1957. "Some Problems in Translating Paragraphs Idiomatically." TBT 8:166-69.

Longacre, Robert E. 1968. *Discourse, Paragraph and Sentence Structure in Selected Philippine Languages.* Vols. I, II, and III. U. S. Department of Health, Education, and Welfare, Office of Education, Institute of International Studies. Santa Ana, Calif.: The Summer Institute of Linguistics.

————. 1972. *Hierarchy and Universality of Discourse Constituents in New Guinea Languages: Discussion.* Washington, D. C.: Georgetown University Press.

Lord, John B. 1964. *The Paragraph, Structure and Style.* New York: Holt, Rinehart and Winston.

Loriot, James, and Hollenbach, Barbara. 1970. "Shipibo Paragraph Structure." *Foundations of Language* 6:43-66.

Miller, Jeanne. 1964. "The Role of Verb Stems in the Mamanwa Kernel Verb Clauses." *Oceanic Linguistics* 3:87-100.

Moore, Bruce and Turner Glen. 1967. "Back-Translation Helps on Mark." NOT 24:1-35.

Nida, Eugene A., and Taber, Charles R. 1969. *The Theory and Practice of Translation.* Leiden, Netherlands: E. J. Brill for the United Bible Societies.

Pike, Kenneth L. 1966. "Tagmemic and Matrix Linguistics Applied to Selected African Languages." Final Report Contract No. OE-5-14-065 U. S. Department of Health, Education, and Welfare, Office of Education, Bureau of Research. Ann Arbor, Mich.: University of Michigan.

Reid, Lawrence Andrew. 1966. *An Ivatan Syntax.* An Oceania Linguistic Monograph, Special publication No. 2. Honolulu: Oceanic Linguistics.

Sheffler, Margaret. 1970. Republication draft. "Mundurkú Discourse."

Stout, Mickey, and Thomson, Ruth. 1971. "Kayapó Narrative." *International Journal of American Linguistics* 37:250-56.

Taber, Charles R. 1966. "The Structure of Sango Narrative." *Hartford Studies in Linguistics* No. 17, Parts I and II. Hartford, Conn.: The Hartford Seminary Foundation.

Wallis, Ethel. 1971. "Discourse Focus in Mezquital Otomi." NOT 42:19-21.

————. 1973. "John's Prologue: Denouement in a Preface." NOT 50:27-29.

Ward, Robert G., and Forster, Jannette. 1967. "Verb Stem Classes in Maranao Transitive Clauses." *Anthropological Linguistics* 9:6:30-42.

Wheatley, James. 1973. "Pronouns and Nominal Elements in Bacairi Discourse." *Linguistics* 104:105-15.

Wonderly, William L. 1968. *Bible Translations for Popular Use.* London: United Bible Societies.

GENERAL INDEX

Nida, Eugene A., 69, 70n
Nonnarrative discourse, 55, 56, 57
NOT (Notes on Translation), 65

Original (language), 26

Parable, 14, 28
Paragraph, 19, 20, 21-25, 26, 55, 57
    argumentative, 21
    explanatory, 21, 24
    hortatory, 21
    narrative, 21, 23
Parallelism, 21, 23
Paraphrase, 23
Participant, 21, 22, 23, 25, 26, 27, 70,
    71, 72, 77, 89
    change of, 36-37
    major, 32-33, 54
    minor, 32-33
    natural introduction of, 32-33
    in quoted material, 37
    role of, 34-35
    tracing of through the discourse,
    33-36, 68
Peak, 27. *See also* Climax
Person
    introduction of, 17
    orientation, 14
Person addressed, involvement of, 17-
    18
Pike, Kenneth L., 18
Positive, 45
Positive-negative, 74
Primary content, 53, 55. *See also*
    Prominence with thematic value
Procedural, 13-14
Prominence
    analysis of, problems connected
    with, 65-68
    definition of, 50
    domain of, 50-51
    with emphasis value, 63-65
    with focus value, 60-63
    with thematic value, 53-60
    signaling devices of, 50, 51
    significance of, in discourse, 52-53

Pronouns, in tracing participants, 35-
    36
Prophecies, 13
Proposition, 10
Propositional analysis, 9, 10
Propositional statement, 10

Quoted speech, 15, 17-18
    direct, 17-18
    indirect, 17-18

Reason, 46, 47
Reid, Lawrence Andrew, 67
Repetition, 23, 72, 74-81
    for amplification, 74-75
    definition of, 74
    functions of, within discourse, 74-81
    as a linking feature, 75-77, 89, 91
    preview and summary, 77-79
    related to lists, 79-80
    to keep theme-line clear, 80-81
Requests, 13
Resolution, 26
Result, 46, 47
Rheme, 58
Role, 68

Secondary content, 55, 56
Sentence, 19-21, 22, 23, 26
    in explanatory discourse, 20
    in hortatory discourse, 20
    in narrative discourse, 20
    terminal, 24, 28
    topic, 22, 57, 82
Sentence length, 15
Setting, 22, 27
    locational, 22, 25
    temporal, 22, 25
Sheffler, Margaret, 55, 83
Singular, for plural, 36
Situation, 25
Specific, 46
State of movement, 22

BIBLICAL INDEX